IB ENGLISH A LANGUAGE & LITERATURE
The Individual Oral

IB English A Language & Literature
The Individual Oral

The Definitive Lang & Lit IO Guide
For the International Baccalaureate [IB] Diploma

Mark Beales

Zouev IB Diploma Publishing

This book is printed on acid-free paper.

Copyright © 2024 Zouev IB Diploma Publishing. All rights reserved.

No part of this book may be used or reproduced in any manner whatsoever without written permission, except in the case of brief quotations embodied in critical articles or reviews.

Published 2024

Printed by Zouev IB Diploma Publishing

ISBN 978-1-7385371-0-5, paperback.

TABLE OF CONTENTS

PART I THE INDIVIDUAL ORAL GUIDE 11

    Welcome to the Individual Oral 12

    What is the Individual Oral (IO)? 12

        What's it worth? 13
        How long does it last? 13
        What do I need to do? 13
        When and where do I do this? 14
        Sounds OK. What if I'm doing Language A: Literature instead? 14

    How is it graded? 15

        Criterion A: Knowledge, understanding and interpretation. 16
        Criterion B: Analysis and evaluation 17
        Criterion C: Focus and organization 18
        Criterion D: Language 19

    What's Literature and What's Language? 20

    Choosing a text 21

    What is a global issue? 22

    How do I come up with a global issue? 24

    Fields of Inquiry 24
    How much help can my teacher give me? 26

    How to prepare for the Individual Oral 26

    Suggested Structure 29

    Sample Individual Oral 34

    Top Ten Tips 39

PART II : TEN EXAMPLES OF EXCELLENT INDIVIDUAL ORAL PRESENTATIONS 43

    1. EXAMPLE ONE (36/40) 45

    2. EXAMPLE TWO (37/40) 51

    3. EXAMPLE THREE (36/40) 55

    4. EXAMPLE FOUR (34/40) 61

    5. EXAMPLE FIVE (37/40) 71

    6. EXAMPLE SIX (38/40) 75

    7. EXAMPLE SEVEN (37/40) 81

    8. EXAMPLE EIGHT (36/40) 85

    9. EXAMPLE NINE (35/40) 93

    10. EXAMPLE TEN (37/40) 101

PART I
THE INDIVIDUAL ORAL GUIDE

Welcome to the Individual Oral

Oral exams tend to fill students with anxiety. What if you dry up? What if you start repeating yourself? What if you don't go on long enough? What if you go on too long?

What if...it all went brilliantly? You walk in prepared and knowing what you're going to say. You impress your teacher with your eloquent delivery and knowledge of the texts. In short, you nail it.

The aim of this guide is to get you to a place where you feel confident and ready for the Individual Oral. It will take considerable effort and planning. It will take hours of reading and researching. But the good news is that I've done this hundreds of times so know exactly what it takes to ace this. As an IB examiner and IB Diploma Coordinator, I've helped many students succeed with the Individual Oral. As well as advice from myself, this guide also contains tips from IB graduates who are happy to pass on their top tips for doing well.

If it does go to plan, and weird as it sounds, these things can go really well, you end up with a top grade but also the belief that you can talk expertly and confidently about a topic, and that's a skill that will last far beyond IB.

What is the Individual Oral (IO)?

First, let's be grateful that you were born around now and not a few years earlier. That's because the previous version of the Language A oral was tough. And stressful.

To give you a quick taster, you would have studied two texts for Standard Level or three at Higher Level. On the day of the test, you are given a random 40-line extract from one of these texts (I used to put these in large brown envelopes, just to add to the drama). You then get 20 minutes to prepare a commentary and, bang, you're off. You had to talk for ten minutes about this extract then answer a few questions from your teacher. Understandably, I had students shaking, trembling and fumbling their way through these ten minutes. Mercifully, IB's latest version of Language A has done away with this.

The new oral is still a challenge, but it's also all in your hands (no brown envelopes or random surprises). You get to prepare as much as you like beforehand and so have far greater control over how your IO will turn out.

What's it worth?
For SL, 30 per cent. For HL, it's worth 20 per cent.

How long does it last?
15 minutes in total. That's ten minutes of you talking and then five minutes of questions from your teacher. It will be recorded (but not videoed).

What do I need to do?

You need to pick a global issue (we'll give you some later on to get you started). You then choose a literary text and a non-literary text that both focus on the same global issue.

You prepare a presentation with two 40-line extracts, one from each text, showing how these texts deal with this global issue. You answer a few questions from your teacher, and you're out of there. The oral is conducted with just your teacher and you present (not in front of an audience or other students).

If you want a little more detail, the guide also asks you to discuss the 'content and form' of these works. We'll get into what that means further down the line.

When and where do I do this?

It's up to your teacher. Of course, you need to have studied a few of the texts first and have to plan and rehearse your oral. The official guide recommends that the oral exam takes place during the end of your first year in the DP or during the first part of the second year.

Your teacher will come up with an assessment schedule for the IO. Some schools will do them all in one day while others may spread it over a few days. As you'll be looking at different global issues and different texts (and get different questions from your teacher), there's no real advantage from doing it before or after your classmates.

Sounds OK. What if I'm doing Language A: Literature instead?

You're in luck. The rules are pretty much the same - the main difference is that you would need to choose two literary texts (with Lang & Lit one text has to be non-literary).

For Literature A, one of the texts has to be written in the language studied and the other from a work in translation.

How is it graded?

IB uses four assessment criteria; they're actually pretty similar for all your Language A assessments so it's worth getting to know them well.

Criterion A Knowledge, understanding and interpretation: 10 marks

Criterion B Analysis and evaluation: 10 marks

Criterion C Focus and organisation: 10 marks

Criterion D Language: 10 marks

Total 40 marks

Students often ask what they need to get a 7. IB marking doesn't quite work like that, as they'll roll all your assessments up into one at the end and only then give it a 1-7 grade. But as a ballpark figure, you would need to get 27 or more to ensure the top grade for the IO.

As a general tip, it's also a waste of your energy to keep chasing the grades and thinking about whether you'll get 28 or 35. Focus on the things you can control, which is your work, and don't worry about the things you can't control, which is what some random examiner gives you at the end of all this. It's tempting to spend a lot of energy and time wondering how to go from a 4 to a 6 in a subject. It's far more useful to think about what skills or knowledge you need to work on; then the grades tend to look after themselves.

For the IO, here's a closer look at how it gets graded:

Criterion A: Knowledge, understanding and interpretation.

How well does the candidate demonstrate knowledge and understanding of the extracts, and of the work and body of work from which they were taken?

To what extent does the candidate make use of knowledge and understanding of the extracts and the work and body of work to draw conclusions in relation to the global issue? How well are ideas supported by references to the extracts, and to the work and body of work?

Marks Level descriptor

0 The work does not reach a standard described by the descriptors below.

1–2 There is little knowledge and understanding of the extracts and the work and body of work in relation to the global issue. References to the extracts and to the work and body of work are infrequent or are rarely appropriate.

3–4 There is some knowledge and understanding of the extracts and the work and body of work in relation to the global issue. References to the extracts and to the work and body of work are at times appropriate.

5–6 There is satisfactory knowledge and understanding of the extracts and the work and body of work and an interpretation of their implications in relation to the global issue. References to the extracts and to the work and body of work are generally relevant and mostly support the candidate's ideas.

7–8 There is good knowledge and understanding of the extracts and the work and body of work and a sustained interpretation of their implications in relation to the global issue. References to the extracts and to the work and body of work are relevant and support the candidate's ideas.

9–10 There is excellent knowledge and understanding of the extracts and of the work and body of work and a persuasive interpretation of their implications in relation to the global issue. References to the extracts and to the work and body of work are well-chosen and effectively support the candidate's ideas.

Criterion B: Analysis and evaluation

How well does the candidate use his or her knowledge and understanding of each of the extracts and their associated work and body of work to analyse and evaluate the ways in which authorial choices present the global issue?

Marks Level descriptor

0 The work does not reach a standard described by the descriptors below.

1–2 The oral is descriptive or contains no relevant analysis. Authorial choices are seldom identified and, if so, are poorly understood in relation to the presentation of the global issue.

3–4 The oral contains some relevant analysis, but it is reliant on description. Authorial choices are identified, but are vaguely treated and/or only partially understood in relation to the presentation of the global issue.

5–6 The oral is analytical in nature, and evaluation of the extracts and their work and body of work is mostly relevant. Authorial choices are identified and reasonably understood in relation to the presentation of the global issue.

7–8 Analysis and evaluation of the extracts and their work and body of work are relevant and at times insightful. There is a good understanding of how authorial choices are used to present the global issue.

9–10 Analysis and evaluation of the extracts and their work and body of work are relevant and Insightful. There is a thorough and nuanced understanding of how authorial choices are used to present the global issue.

Criterion C: Focus and organization

How well does the candidate deliver a structured, well-balanced and focused oral?

How well does the candidate connect ideas in a cohesive manner?

Marks Level descriptor

0 The work does not reach a standard described by the descriptors below.

1–2 The oral rarely focuses on the task. There are few connections between ideas.

3–4 The oral only sometimes focuses on the task, and treatment of the extracts, and of the work and body of work, may be unbalanced. There are some connections between ideas, but these are not always coherent.

5–6 The oral maintains a focus on the task, despite some lapses; treatment of the extracts and work and body of work is mostly balanced. The development of ideas is mostly logical; ideas are generally connected in a cohesive manner.

7–8 The oral maintains a mostly clear and sustained focus on the task; treatment of the extracts and work and body of work is balanced. The development of ideas is logical; ideas are cohesively connected in an effective manner.

9–10 The oral maintains a clear and sustained focus on the task; treatment of the extracts and work and body of work is well-balanced. The development of ideas is logical and convincing; ideas are connected in a cogent manner.

Criterion D: Language

How clear, accurate and effective is the language?

Marks Level descriptor

0 The work does not reach a standard described by the descriptors below.

1–2 The language is rarely clear or accurate; errors often hinder communication. Vocabulary and syntax are imprecise and frequently inaccurate. Elements of style (for example, register, tone and rhetorical devices) are inappropriate to the task and detract from the oral.

3–4 The language is generally clear; errors sometimes hinder communication. Vocabulary and syntax are often imprecise with inaccuracies. Elements of style (for example, register, tone and rhetorical devices) are often inappropriate to the task and detract from the oral.

5–6 The language is clear; errors do not hinder communication. Vocabulary and syntax are appropriate to the task but simple and repetitive. Elements of style (for example, register, tone and rhetorical devices) are appropriate to the task and neither enhance nor detract from the oral.

7–8 The language is clear and accurate; occasional errors do not hinder communication. Vocabulary and syntax are appropriate and varied. Elements of style (for example, register, tone and rhetorical devices) are appropriate to the task and somewhat enhance the oral.

9–10 The language is clear, accurate and varied; occasional errors do not hinder communication. Vocabulary and syntax are varied and create an effect. Elements of style (for example, register, tone and rhetorical devices) are appropriate to the task and enhance the oral.

Criterion D: Language

What's Literature and What's Language?

IB's rules about what is literary and what's non-literary are worth getting your head around. Most of the time it's obvious what's literary: Shakespeare, Orwell and Achebe, and so on. But what if Achebe wrote a letter? That's literary cos he's a literary figure. What if you're using one of Obama's anti-gun speeches? Also literary as it's of literary merit and from someone known for their use of rhetoric. What if you want to use a speech by Donald Trump? You can see where this is going. There are some definite shades of grey here but don't let that worry you - ask your teacher for advice, and if they're not sure they can always ask IB.

One other quirk worth knowing - if you're using a music video and discussing the cinematography and visuals it's non-literary but if you're looking at the lyrics of someone who's on IB's 'prescribed reading list', like Kendrick Lamar, that would be literary.

In fact, the reading list makes it pretty simple to pick a literary author. If your writer is on this, they're literary. Job done. If they're not on the list but are clearly literary writers, that's also pretty simple. John Steinbeck isn't on the reading list but he's obviously literary. Why isn't such a literary giant on the list, you may ask (and many teachers have done just that)? We think we know the answer and it has nothing to do with Steinbeck's literary merits and more to do with how examiners long for something to grade that isn't Of Mice and Men.

The main thing is don't have two literary texts or two non-literary texts. Examples of this would be a graphic novel and song lyrics (both literary) or a music video / advertisement combo (both non-literary).

Choosing a text

One of the hardest parts of the IO (aside from actually delivering it) is deciding which texts to use. And then what the global issue is that will glue them both together.

Your starting point may well be the global issue itself, because the whole oral is about how your texts represent and explore it.

You need to pick two extracts that are no more than 40 lines long. If you have a longer poem, pick the section that gives you the most to discuss (you can't cut and paste the best parts of a poem either; the 40 lines have to be continuous). Make sure the name of the text and its author are given near the top.

You can bring these texts into the exam room, along with your Outline, but the texts cannot be annotated in any way. This also means there's no point memorising long quotes - they'll be right in front of you so you won't impress the examiner by just reciting long sections (much better to say 'in lines 7-10 we can see how the author begins to…') This saves you time, avoids looking like you're padding out the time, and makes you sound more like a literary student.

Literary texts are often part of a bigger piece of work, like a short story or play. If that's the case you'll also need to build in some time to talk about how the global issue is represented in the rest of that work. This is probably the one area where students fall down on most - they only focus on the extracts in front of them and, while it's tough to pack everything into ten minutes, it's vital that you talk about the wider work at some point.

When you talk about the non-literary text, you also need to build in time to talk about the author's bigger body of work. If you pick an advertisement, talk about some of the author's other adverts - these could come from the same campaign or other texts by the same agency. If you're looking at a photograph, also talk about other images by the same author/photographer. If you're looking at a newspaper article, you should really discuss other articles by the same writer (it may be tempting to just find other articles from the same newspaper, but these may not have the same 'voice' or represent the global issue in the same way). If you're using editorials it's easier as they are said to be the voice of the newspaper and you could argue they will be similar in tone and view. Either way, if there's any doubt about who the 'author' is, make it clear near the start how you plan to define this.

An interesting aspect of this assessment is that students don't have to study the same texts - there is much more freedom for you to make your own choices. All the works used for the oral must have been studied and discussed in class. IB uses the phrase 'studied and discussed' to allow teachers some freedom to interpret that as they wish.

And remember that students need to study the equivalent of a full-length work to count that as a 'work'. So, for example, if you're looking at short stories you would need to think about their length and complexity and how many would be the same as, say, a novel. The same goes for poems, advertisements, etc.

What is a global issue?

It may seem obvious, but IB has a few rules about what it thinks is a global issue. First up, it needs to be significant on a big scale. Not just some minor local thing.

Next up, it has to be 'transnational'. Occasionally, students will focus on an issue that only really affects one country or has texts from the same country (which, in itself is ok, but you'd have to show that the issue went further than that).

Lastly, its impact must be felt in 'everyday local contexts'.

I'd add a couple more of my own suggestions. Don't make it too broad as issues like 'feminism' or 'racism' are just too big to cover adequately in ten minutes. Far better to look at 'the effect of racism on education' or 'the power of the media in defining beauty'.

Also, remember that the issue doesn't have to be a negative one. True, bad news does sell and global issues do tend to be downers, but there's nothing to stop you going with a positive global issue.

How do I come up with a global issue?

This is where your learner portfolio is useful. The portfolio is like a sketchpad; it's your chance to collect notes and ideas as you go along. Although it isn't assessed or submitted, it's also a requirement. Many of my students make blog-style pages but it could be in a notebook or anywhere you feel comfortable.

Once you've decided on the platform you prefer, you can use the learner portfolio to keep a note of possible global issues. As you discover new texts, think about which global issues they could be linked with and also which texts may work well together. I always find it fascinating to see how students create links I'd never thought of, from Instagram pages to photographic documentaries; the possibilities are endless so don't be afraid to be a bit creative and go beyond the obvious.

Pick out a phrase or an image and then group them together with those from other texts. Do they have the same message (content) but deliver it in different ways (form)?

It's also your portfolio, which means it's your chance to create your own texts, develop your own thoughts, and show your planning (it's not just Maths' teachers who say this).

Your Language A course talks about 'fields of inquiry'. These are broad areas of interest that you can use to spark some ideas into life; if there's enough of a flame they may also develop into a global issue. Note that you don't have to use these - they're just there to help.

Fields of Inquiry

Culture, identity and community

This could look at how texts represent class, nationality, religion, gender and sexuality and how these affect society. Other options could include colonialism and migration.

Beliefs, values and education

Here you could look at how texts explore societies' values and how this forms our communities.

When there is conflict between different values, you may like to see how those tensions play out and are represented in texts.

Politics, power and justice

This is a very broad field of inquiry that goes beyond governments and also looks at equality and inequality, human rights and the gap between rich and poor.

Art, creativity and the imagination

A particular popular field, this one touches on what inspires us, beauty and the function and value of art in our world. If you're starting to think these all sound like possible Theory of Knowledge lessons, then you're right. TOK gets everywhere.

Science, technology and the environment

Finally, you could look at people and technology and the benefits or threats these pose. Or you could combine them and look at technology and the media (could AI end up writing a book on how to do your oral, for example?)

How much help can my teacher give me?

Teachers can help you choose which texts may work well and whether your global issue is a good one or not. They can also give you practice orals and give you feedback on these, usually with a focus on the assessment criteria. They can also go through your outline and give you tips. One thing they cannot do is practice your actual oral with you.

And you only get one crack at this, which is why the oral can add some pressure to your studies. You can't go back and do it again (even if your practice oral was awesome and your real one was just ok - it's the real one that is submitted).

One other rule that's worth knowing - you can't use the same material for the oral and your Extended Essay. That's known as double-dipping and IB frowns upon that kind of thing.

How to prepare for the Individual Oral

Let's next look at how you can begin planning for the IO. We should say here that there are several approaches and you'll need to figure out what works best for you.

One way in is to choose a key moment in the work you have studied. Think about what makes it important and how it links to a wider issue in society (the fields of inquiry are very handy for working this out).

Next, think about the author. This is especially important if you're dealing with a piece of fiction. Those characters probably aren't real, so don't treat them like they are. Instead, focus on the writer who created them and, crucially, why he or she created them. Ask yourself:

- Is the author presenting a particular issue?
- How does the author choose to present it?
- What 'authorial' decisions have been made here?
- What techniques has the author used and what effect do they have on the reader?

Go beyond literally what's happening and think about why it stands out. By focusing on your reaction and understanding why you reacted in that way, you can usually start to think about what the author did to create that emotion. As you build up this picture, you can think more widely and consider other texts that you've studied. Ask yourself if they create similar reactions - if they do, you may be on to something that could be developed into a global issue.

Another way of starting is with the global issue itself. There may be a particular area you have a personal interest in and want that to be your focus. If that's the case, narrow down the global issue as much as possible and then consider which texts are the best examples of this. This takes quite a lot of creativity and imagination in order to find texts that work well here but, hey, that's what Language A is all about.

Take some time here as it's vital you get this part right. Once you're happy with it, you can start thinking about how to plan your IO. I'd suggest analysing each extract in detail is a good move - highlight, mindmap, colour code, whatever works for you. Dig deep into the text (use those fancy technical terms your teacher told you) and really understand how it works. If you're using images or video, be sure that you also understand their form and the technical jargon that's connected with them. In the example you'll see later, I did this with a couple of texts. My focus wasn't on simply analysing each text; all the while I was thinking more about how each text dealt with the global issue. Once I had fully understood this, I was ready to plan out the oral itself. For this, the Outline is ideal. Here's a version that I've used in the past.

Individual Oral Outline

List a maximum of 10 points that will show how your Individual Oral will be structured. An official form will be provided later.

Global Issue	
Texts Chosen	Literary: Non-literary:

Notes for the oral (maximum of 10)
1
2
3
4
5

6
7
8
9
10

Suggested Structure

How do you fill in an Outline? Again, there are numerous ways but I'd suggest there are some essentials that all good orals will have. These will be an introduction (like a trailer for your oral), a section where you analyse the extracts, the wider bodies of work, and a conclusion. Here's a suggested structure in a bit more detail:

1. Introduce your global issue

2. Introduce your literary and non-literary texts, and make it clear where they come from

3. Add some relevant context about the global issue. Start to bring in your two texts.

4. A thesis statement, showing how you'll link both texts to the global issue.

5. Literary text: explain your key points from your Outline. Remember to refer to the wider literary work too. Link this to the global issue.

6. Non-literary text: explain your key points from your Outline. Remember to refer to some of the other non-literary works by this author too. Link this to the global issue.

7. Compare how the lit and non-lit texts discuss the global issue.

8. Conclusion: what have these two texts helped us learn about the global issue?

Let's make this a little more specific. Below are some planning docs I used when I did a sample oral, just to try and put myself in my students' shoes and understand what was needed. Further on there's a transcript of the actual oral, which was based on Dove's Campaign for Real Beauty and the Carol Ann Duffy poem Medusa.

First up there's a planning doc I give students with some useful questions designed to make sure you hit the key points. Following that is an Outline I created - note how brief some points are; they're simply there to help remind me of the points I want to make.

INDIVIDUAL ORAL PLANNING DOC

Student Name: _____

Chosen literary text	Medusa – Carol Ann Duffy	Chosen literary extract of 40 lines (provide a link if possible)	Whole poem
Chosen non-literary text	Dove – Real Beauty	Chosen non-literary extract of 40 lines (provide a link if possible)	Whole advert (part of a Body of Work)
What global issue are your texts linked to?	The representation of female beauty in western culture.		
How is your global issue important on a wide scale?	It affects many women who may feel discriminated against because of their physical appearance, and how society judges them because of this.		
How is your global issue transnational?	The representation of women's beauty is something that appears in many advertisements across many countries. Equally, Duffy's complaint that her lover has left her for someone more beautiful could resonate with women, who have formed relationships based largely on their physical appearance. It also links with the control men have in patriarchal societies, and continue to have, despite increasing awareness over feminism.		
How is your global issue something that is felt in everyday local contexts?	The issue is also a highly personal one, as women see adverts on social media every day that use persuasive devices to give them a narrow definition of beauty.		

How will you show how your global issue is presented through the **content** of each work?	Through the advert, the form is important as it counters traditional adverts that use models, who tend to conform to a narrow version of beauty.
How will you show how your global issue is presented through the **form** of each work?	Duffy's poem is irregular and disjointed. This form reflects the anger and resentment felt by the speaker. The enjambment and lack of rhyme scheme also reflects these emotions. The advert's form challenges the normal tropes of beauty advertising by using older models, or models with 'flaws'.

Individual Oral Outline

List a maximum of 10 points that will show how your Individual Oral will be structured. An official form will be provided later.

Global Issue	The representation of female beauty in society
Texts Chosen	Literary: 'Medusa' – Carol Ann Duffy Non-literary: Dove Campaign for Real Beauty

Notes for the oral (maximum of 10)
1 Introduce the global issue: the representation of female beauty in society
2

	Introduce texts and add context about the global issue.
3	A thesis statement, linking both texts to the global issue. Both texts deal with female beauty but in different ways – one shows us the unfair way in which men cast aside older women in favour of younger ones; the other presents an alternative version of beauty, that seems to be more internal.
4	Start to discuss the content of the texts. Duffy's poem – purpose is to challenge her husband (and the reader) to deal with her loss of perceived 'beauty' and explain her anger. Dove challenges the reader to see different kinds of 'beauty' and embrace this, free from relationships.
5	Duffy: language and tone points
6	Dove: purpose, language and tone points
7	Discuss the form of both poems
8	How do both texts discuss the global issue?

9	Comment on other texts by the authors. Havisham deals with the loss of a love and blames men. Other poems represent women in a more powerful light – Mrs Aesop ('By Christ, he could bore for purgatory') and Anne Hathaway. Dove 'wrinkled/wonderful?' 'beauty spots / ugly spots?'
10	Conclusion: what have these two texts helped us learn about the global issue? Both texts challenge the concept of traditional beauty. Medusa angrily demands attention from her unfaithful husband, who is interested in younger forms of beauty, while Dove highlights imperfections and suggests they can be beautiful. Duffy: furiously turns everything to grey stone, reflecting her lost beauty. Dove: offers more of an olive branch and suggests grey can be positive.

Sample Individual Oral

I'll walk you through an example I did to understand what the process was like. In this section, I'll explain my thought process and, while everyone's approach will be different, I hope this gives you one way of approaching the oral. The numbers here correspond to the numbers in my Outline.

1) My talk today will focus on an important global issue – the representation of female beauty in society. The #Metoo movement and a rise in feminist ideals has prompted extra awareness about women's rights. Traditional notions of 'beauty' are being challenged, and this prompted me to consider these two texts.

2) My first text is Carol Ann Duffy's 'Medusa', taken from her collection 'The World's Wife' and a non-literary text, an advertisement from Dove's Campaign for Real Beauty. Both these texts focus closely on how female beauty is represented in society, but in very different ways. One similarity though is that they both challenge the reader to see 'beauty' in a broader sense and not be restrained by societal ideals and stereotypes.

3) In this presentation, I will first discuss the purpose and tone of the literary, then non-literary, texts. This will be followed by a close reading of both texts, and then an analysis of their conclusions.

My thesis is that both texts deal with female beauty but in significantly different ways – one shows us the unfair way in which men cast aside older women in favour of younger, more beautiful ones; the other presents an alternative version of beauty that seems to be more internalised and less concerned with relationships with men.

4) To begin with, we will explore 'Medusa'. The purpose of the poem is to reflect the speaker's sorrow and then rage through a dramatic monologue as she finds herself abandoned by her lover, or husband.

5) The speaker is consumed with fury following her husband's cheating, which seems to have occurred once the wife has aged and lost her conventional 'beauty' or attractiveness. As a result, there is a growing anger, which can be seen in the development of the nouns 'a suspicion, a doubt, a jealousy' and later in the verbs when the speaker says she 'glanced', then 'looked' and finally 'stared' at objects that she turned to stone. We sense her growing frustration at being abandoned as she leaves behind traditional forms of beauty, evident in the alliterative line 'My bride's breath soured, stank / in the grey bags of my lungs'. She was

once a 'bride' in white, connoting her purity, but this has now changed to being 'yellow fanged', which connotes decay and ageing.

Duffy alludes to the story of Medusa, who could turn her victims to stone by looking at them. When she talks about 'bullet tears in my eyes' the connotations of violence is clear. Bullets, and her own eyes, can be used to kill. She suggests that men will inevitably look for more beautiful options when she says, in a resigned tone 'I know you'll go, betray me, stray from home'.

The poem then employs stark imagery to describe the power that derives from her anger. We see how the 'birds and the bees' – a clear reference to her crumbling sex life – are turned to stone. The harsh sounds of 'pebble, spattered and shattered' reflect her anger, while the cat rolling in a 'heap of shit' seems to symbolise her new, lonely life.

The poem ends in a pleading, plaintive way as the speaker reminds her love, repeatedly, of 'your girls, your girls' and then refers directly to her former beauty as she asks, rhetorically 'wasn't I beautiful / wasn't I fragrant and young?'

The tone of the poem is at first regretful, but soon turns to anger as the speaker resents how society treats women who lose their beauty. Duffy takes this to an extreme by creating a persona based on a classically horrific figure, but then as Andrew Dworkin claimed, women are often portrayed as the root of all evil, from Eve in the Garden of Eden to the jealous witches and step-mothers of fairy tales. By the end of the poem, the tone can be read as being out for revenge, as the speaker uses an imperative to demand 'Look at me now'. This at first appears to remind us of the older state she is in 'now', however it could be seen as a final plea to her husband. Given that she is Medusa, however, it can be read as a threat, as by looking directly at her she will gain her revenge and he will be turned to stone.

6) The Dove text also appeals to the intended reader to see beauty in a different light. We see the older model smiling and are then immediately presented with a false dilemma: is she 'grey' or 'gorgeous'? The voting-style boxes suggest there are only two options, which reflects the overly-simplified view of female beauty prevalent in society.

The rhetorical question 'why can't more women feel glad to be grey?' alludes to the LGBTQ slogan of 'glad to be gay', which gives the text a light, appealing tone. The imperative that follows 'Join the beauty debate' is a call to action that assumes there is a debate taking place – the link to the company's website clearly suggests the reader should now go there to give their own views.

Looking at the image itself, it is shot slightly from below, giving the model an empowering look. She is smiling confidently, while her grey hair contrasts with the black, non-imposing clothing she wears.

As a result, the tone is uplifting and upbeat, and the ethical message from Dove suggests the readers should have a similar attitude towards unconventional forms of female beauty.

7) The form of both poems is important. Duffy's poem is irregular and disjointed. This form reflects the anger and resentment felt by the speaker. The enjambments also reflects these emotions. Duffy uses half-rhymes 'terrified / eyes' and internal rhymes 'I know you'll go' does give the poem some unity, however. Structurally, the stanzas are similar, apart from the single-line final one, which makes its message all the more stark.

Dove's advert is also irregular, in the sense that it goes against the normal tropes of beauty advertising. By using older models, it is directly challenging the usual younger models used, and by doing so suggests it is taking an ethical stance against the representation of female beauty.

8) As a result of both texts, we can see how female beauty is often represented in a simplistic, narrow way. The result, in Duffy's case, is a man who buys into this desire for someone 'beautiful' and abandons someone who truly loved him. With Dove, we see how 'beauty' can have many faces and should not be limited to one narrow definition.

9) This stance can also be seen in similar adverts in the same campaign. Dove uses older models in other adverts – one asks if the woman is 'wrinkled' or 'wonderful', while it also has images of imperfections, one questioning if blemishes are 'beauty spots' or 'ugly spots'.

In Duffy's other poems, especially Havisham, she again portrays a female victim dealing with the loss of a love, who blames men's frailties. Other poems, however, represent women in a far more powerful light – Mrs Aesop has the mocking line 'By Christ, he could bore for purgatory', while in Anne Hathaway, Duffy allows the speaker to take ownership of her more famous husband in an affectionate manner.

10) In conclusion, then, we can see how both texts allow us to learn something about the global issue of female beauty and representation.

Both texts challenge the concept of traditional beauty and the possible misogynistic values placed on it. Medusa angrily demands attention from her unfaithful husband, who is interested in younger forms of beauty, while Dove highlights imperfections and suggests they can be beautiful.

The texts themselves arrive at different conclusions. Duffy's speaker furiously turns everything to grey stone, reflecting her lost beauty and passions. Dove directly offers more of an olive branch, embracing the 'grey' of older beauty, and suggesting it can be just as stunning.

How would this have scored? Pretty well, as it has a clear global issue that isn't just 'feminism' and analyses both texts fairly thoroughly, given the time constraints. Given more time, I would have liked to expand on the wider bodies of work section to give the oral more balance but, overall, it's a decent oral and would score towards the top end of each criterion.

Top Ten Tips

1) One of the best ways to understand the oral is to listen to others. Not just those who get straight 7s, but also what a 4 or a 5 sound like. IB has released several samples and your teacher will have access to these on the MyIB site. After listening, pretend you're an examiner and try grading it. When examiners do this, they use a 'best-fit' approach. This means you look at a criterion and then the descriptions. Keep reading the descriptions until you get to one that's a little too good for the work you're marking. Drop back to the previous description and, bingo, that's the grade you're after. Of course, sometimes there are grey areas so you need to think carefully about which description is the most appropriate. When marking your oral, examiners have some guidelines to help. These say that a work doesn't have to be absolutely faultless to get the top score in a particular area. Examiners also don't think about a 'pass' or 'fail' or even an overall grade; they simply mark each section as best they can. Also, each of these criteria is graded separately, so you could do well in one or

two areas but poorly in others. Examiners don't listen to your oral and go 'oh, that's a 5'. They focus only on these criteria and, later on, IB will decide how to convert your 33 out of 40 into a 1-7 grade.

2) Have a balance. You need to talk about the literary and non-literary texts for roughly the same amount of time. You also need to talk about the wider bodies of work that both come from. So that's basically four parts. Students sometimes focus on their first text too heavily, usually for fear of finishing early. They then overdo it and don't have room for much else. Or they focus so much on the 40-line extracts they don't leave room for a wider discussion about the bodies of work. That's where planning and the Outline come to your rescue. Here, you can map out in advance what you'll be doing, and when. It's not an exact science and you shouldn't plan this down to the last second. You also don't have to talk about everything completely equally (nearly everyone discusses the extracts in detail and spends less time on the wider works, which is fine). Just be aware of this, because having a balance is an easy way to pick up some points.

3) You need to practise, even if you're a native speaker. Just because you can speak fluently and eloquently, it doesn't guarantee you a 7. Assuming your language skills will get you by would be a huge mistake. If you don't do the groundwork you won't have anything of substance to talk about.

4) The global issue is at the heart of all this. When you're in the exam room you'll have your two extracts staring back at you. Sometimes, it's tempting to focus only on those and forget that your real job is to talk about how the global issue crops up in

both. But it's not an after-thought; it has to be front and centre, so don't describe the texts in detail without linking them to the global issue.

5) Spend time getting your intro right. Too often, students race through this in a desire to get to the meat of the discussion. But you need a little appetiser first. Explain the global issue (especially if it's not obvious) and briefly say how the texts deal with it. If you need to justify who an 'author' is for your extracts, do it here.

6) Pace yourself. Running out of things to say after seven minutes is going to give you a problem. In terms of criterion C (organisation), you'll lose marks, and it also means you're going to get eight minutes of questions, rather than the usual five. Given that you control the first part of the oral but not the second, that doesn't put you in a strong position. You have a chance to rehearse the oral and, when you do, keep a close eye on the clock.

7) Don't stress about the questions. Yes, you don't know what's coming but your teacher isn't looking to catch you out. When I'm the assessor, I'll have a few stock questions ready to use, but I rarely get to them. Instead, I listen to the student and look for areas where they could expand more or where they simply haven't covered enough areas ('tell me more about the wider body of work' is probably my most-common question). The questions should aim to help you plug any gaps, so think of them as your friend.

8) To AI or not AI? That's the question for many students, who may be getting various answers from various teachers. IB has a clear policy about this, which says it's fine to use AI as a guide but any time you use it, you have to cite it, in the same way you would any source. Personally, when I've used it I've found it pretty ineffective for this kind of task.

9) Get ready early. OK, so time management is a massive part of IB life in general, but for the oral you'll need to give your extracts to your teacher at least a week ahead of the assessment. That's so your teacher can check the extracts are appropriate and also to help them prepare questions for you.

10) Finally, be assertive. Students who go in feeling confident tend to do well. Don't be timid and worry about what you don't know. The point of the oral and, indeed, every assessment is to reward you for what you do know. Plan things carefully, rehearse fully and then you will nail it.

PART II
TEN EXAMPLES OF EXCELLENT INDIVIDUAL ORAL PRESENTATIONS

The IO scripts featured in this section are all recently presented IO that scored exceptionally well (band 7) after being moderated by the IBO. Where possible, actual examiner feedback has been included. The IO scripts are presented in the exact same way as they were written, without any edits or changes to formatting. We do not retain the copyright of these IO, nor is this publication endorsed by the IBO. The IO are being re-printed with the permission of the original authors.

FOR COPYRIGHT REASONS, WE ARE UNABLE TO INCLUDE THE ORIGINAL TEXTS.

Please refer to these online.

1. EXAMPLE ONE (36/40)

Title: Examining Toni Morrison's *The Bluest Eye*

and four of Nelson Mandela's speeches

Author: CK

Session: May 2022

Level: English L&L HL

"Hello, today in my IO I will be exploring the global issue: Politics, power and justice, by focusing on the dehumanization of the less powerful. I will explore it through Toni Morrison's novel *The Bluest Eye*, which reveals the dehumanization of black people in white centric America, and Mandela's speeches which reveal the dehumanization of the less powerful black south Africans living under the racist apartheid regime. In the novel Morrison whose purpose is to humanize black people reveals how the powerless are unable to prevent being dehumanized, and in response internalize that dehumanization or project it onto others. On the other hand Mandela depicts the dehumanization of the powerless as a means to garner support from his audience for his purpose of fighting against their apartheid oppressors.

Starting off with the literary body of work. According to Claudia, a fellow African American, Cholly rapes his daughter by the end of the novel. And thus has "joined the animals, an old dog, a snake, a ratty n word". The **tricolon,** of comparisons to animals and a derogatory term used to sell black people as commodities emphasizes to readers that Cholly is more animal than human or devoid of humanity. This causes readers to dehumanize him, despite knowing very little about him. And is something he is powerless in preventing.

This dehumanization is further seen zooming in to the literary extract. In the extract Cholly and Darlene, are caught by two white men when having sexual intercourse. Morrison highlights the imbalance of power as whilst Cholly addresses the men with "sir" in line 10, which has connotations of respect, Cholly is told "come on coon." and "to get on wid it" in line 27 and 9. The comparison to an animal and the **colloquialism** of the men's **dialogue**, makes clear to the readers that the men do not respect Cholly's privacy nor dignity as a human. The demanding and direct **tone** also shows readers, that the white men even feel entitled to using Cholly for their sexual entertainment. Again, this highlights to readers how Cholly is violated, loses power over his body, and is thus dehumanized by the more powerful white men.

Continuing still with the extract, As the dehumanization continues, Cholly becomes increasingly helpless and hateful towards Darlene. In the beginning of the extract, Cholly's first thought in line 2 was whether " he had hurt her," this is **juxtaposed** to how Cholly In an attempt to control and have power over his humiliation attempts to pull "her dress up" in line 19 and sees her as a monster with baby claws. This **diction** and juxtaposition between treatment towards Darlene reveals how he starts to project the dehumanization onto Darlene as a means to cope with the his dehumanization. However all of Cholly's attempts to have power is effortlessly invalidated through the whitemen's eerie harrowing laugh "heee heee hee," in lines 7, 24, and 26. The **repetition** of the interrupting **onomatopoeia** develops a desperate tone highlights Cholly's powerlessness.

Connecting back to the body of work, for readers who in the beginning of the novel felt justified to dehumanize him, this extract offers a reason for his actions, though unjustified, is a product of the society that dehumanizes him. This fulfils Morrisons goal of prompting the predominantly white readers to recognize how they are a part of the problem by dehumanizing people like Cholly, as they did in the beginning of the novel.

Now going back to the body of work, Morrison expands on feeling dehumanized when describing how Polly was birthing Pecola. Despite Polly being in pain and a powerless pregnant lady, the doctors joked that black women "don't have any trouble with delivering…as they deliver right away. The comparison to an animal and **diction** "any trouble" and right away", creates a effortless tone despite the painful process of giving birth. This makes clear how the doctors dismiss, deprive, and invalidate polly's option to even voice out discomfort or any sort of human emotion. This suggests to readers that Polly loses autonomy over her voice and treatment as a human being, highlighting how Polly is dehumanized.

Dehumanization is seen again in Pecola, a little powerless black girl. According to Claudia all the abuse and racism or "waste" of society was all "dumped on her and which she absorbed." The metaphor makes clear to readers how Pecola claims dehumanization as a part of her very being. The internalization allows Pecola to be a scapegoat for society including the black community, as through dehumanizing Pecola they felt wholesome, beautiful, more human. This highlights to black readers how they too are responsible for the dehumanization of the least powerful, prompting them to start humanizing and furthering Morrison's purpose .

Now moving on to the non-literary work. In the extract from Mandela speech "I am prepared to die" Mandela reveals how society leaves black South Africans powerless over their life and dehumanized. Mandela's **diction** of "policy" in line 1 and "Legislation" and in line 2 that result, preserve, and entrenches "black inferiority" in lines 1 and 2, makes clear to the audience that the powerlessness black people face is the product of the apartheid system, it is systemic and official. Mandela strengthens this notion through the example of pass laws. As in line 12 they "render any African liable to police surveillance at any time." This makes clear how the apartheid system that govern south african society renders black south Africans powerless and dehumanized, as they produce laws such as the pass law that strip their right to autonomy and privacy.

Mandela expands, explaining the impacts of such dehumanization in the anaphora in lines 27 to 36 through the inclusion of phrases such as wanting to perform work which they are capable of doing" and "travel the country." in lines 28 and 35. This makes clear to Mandela's white audience how black south Africans are deprived of things considered basic human rights, highlighting how black south African are dehumanized from basic human life and wants. Moreover, the repetition of "Africans want" and the synthetic pronoun "we want" provides Mandela's audience with a feeling of reclaiming their power through a sense of comradery being apart of "we". This reclamation is furthered through the repetition of high modality language and antithesis in the anaphora through "we want" and not". for example Mandela says "Africans want to be allowed out after 11' o clock at night and not be confined to their rooms" This highlight that whilst black south Africans are currently dehumanized and powerless under the apartheid regime, they can take charge of their life, like going out at night when they choose to do so. In this way Mandela prompts African listeners to yearn for that power and humanization and thus persuades them to fight against their oppressors that exploit their powerlessness, furthering his purpose of fighting the apartheid regime.

Expanding to the body of work Mandela similarly prompts his listeners to fight against the apartheid regime through depictions of dehumanization of the powerless. In No Easy Walk to Freedom Mandela lists how in "homes" and "schools," and a seemingly endless list of places black people discuss the misdeeds like "inhuman exploitation" and "grinding poverty" of the apartheid regime . The lists and imagery, develops a desperate tone that appeals to the African audience who relate, but also highlights to his more powerful white audience of how the oppression is an occurrence everywhere and all the time.

Similarly, In We Shall crush apartheid Mandela, through more imagery, reveals how "ferocious fire pouring a hail of bullets killing hundreds of black men, women and children. The imagery and mention of the aggressive, merciless and senseless murder of black people and children, which have connotations of innocence and fragility, characterizes the apartheid regime as an evil system that does not care for the nation's future, their children.

Finally, even after Mandela is finally inaugurated as South Africa as president, in his inauguration Mandela continues to communicate how the "racism and racist oppression" has caused a "festering sore". This gruesome metaphor and the previous violent imagery discussed previously is juxtaposed to how he explains working towards fighting apartheid and reclaiming African power has allowed for a "rainbow nation" full of human dignity. The rainbow has connotations with hope and symbolizes a nation comprised of many skin colours. This juxtaposition of happy and hopeful imagery and aggressive imagery makes clear to listeners how an Africa that humanizes the less powerful, is a step in the right direction, prompting his listeners to be inspired and continue their fight against the apartheid.

To conclude, while both address the dehumanization of the less powerful in different ways, it is clear that the black people living in both south African and America are easily dehumanized due to their powerlessness within society either systemically or socially. Both Morrison and Mandela use stylistic and structural choices to humanize the dehumanized and challenge their audience to make a change. For Morrison's readers it's to humanize those easily dehumanized, and for Mandela's audience its inspiration to reclaim their power and humanity by fighting the oppressive apartheid regime. Thank you."

2. EXAMPLE TWO (37/40)

Title: The relevance of mental health stigmas in eventuating self-actualisation

Author: Anonymous

Session: November 2023

Level: English L&L SL

Mental illness is a topic now broadly discussed in modern-day society, although uncommonly acknowledged in the 20th century. During this period in time, there seemed to be a global stigma around mental health, often leading those with the illness to create facades, further influencing their potential of self-actualisation. Now, I will take the time to elaborate on this issue, specifically looking at the literary text, 'Mrs Dalloway' and an extract from the final pages of the novel. This is a novel written by the modernist author, Virginia Woolf, in 1925. I will also review the non-literary poem written by Ted Hughes, 'Your Paris', in 1998; despite both texts being written decades apart, it is apparent that persistent mental health stigmas continue to prevail in literature and provide relevant insight and scopes for the audience to address the issue.

'Mrs Dalloway', as a whole, embodies the mental struggles faced by the characters Septimus and Clarissa; although both face incredibly different positions in society - Clarissa being an elite, older woman of society and Septimus being a young, male war-veteran - there are many parallels shown between their mentality and how they attempt to cope with them. In showing that both characters experience differing circumstances, Woolf connects to the global issue by describing that any person can encounter mental illness and must deal with it in ways that conform to society. To do this, Woolf employs her self-coined 'tunneling' technique throughout the novel, in which the transition between the perspectives of different characters flows smoothly and is written in a 'stream of consciousness'. Woolf herself suffered from a bipolar disorder and likely inserted aspects of her own illness into this 'tunneling' technique, paralleling them to frequent shifts within the interior thoughts of numerous characters. This unstructured method of writing is characteristic of the modernist movement, which is known to have marked an age of crisis and mutual sense of loss, exile and alienation, all of which describes the context of the era where the mental health stigma was commonly present.

Furthermore, the motif of Shakespeare's work is often referenced throughout the novel and describes the survival of introspection in a period where emotional and mental sensitivity was criticised. Both Clarissa and Septimus are shown to greatly appreciate Shakespeare's works, often quoting lines from his play *Othello*, although Septimus was shown to lose his solace in poetry after returning with shell-shock from the war. It is made evident throughout the novel that characters who did not appreciate poetry as Clarissa and Septimus did found themselves unable to emotionally express themselves. This suggests that Clarissa and Septimus, both struggling with mental illness, are actually able to experience a greater sense of self-actualisation than others who comply with the mental health stigma.

I will be analysing the moment in the novel where Woolf describes a climactic scene within Clarissa's party. In lines 1 and 2, Clarissa is described as having been drawn *'into the shelter of a common femininity'*, consequently explaining the context of their setting, where a *'sheltered'* feminine role is expected to be upheld to conform with traditionalist views; that is, remain where they are, to hold back from expressing their true individuality. This notion is disrupted as she hears about Septimus' suicide, lines 4 to 6; in a time where England prided themselves on those who served to protect in the army, the suicide of a young veteran would have shocked the general public, displaying the reality of how society viewed and treated mental health. Although startled, Clarissa manages a small exclamation to this news, personifying death as an uninvited guest to her party. The intrusion of death is Woolf's method of describing a metaphor for Clarissa's mental state, where thoughts concerning death may occasionally and unexpectedly enter her mind as she attempts to connect and blend in with a society which does not concern itself with mental health. This is reinforced in line 8, where the 'tunnelling technique' is disrupted by truncated sentences, also a metaphor for the emptiness in Clarissa's mind. Her described sympathy for Septimus' suicide in lines 15 and 16 displays how even Clarissa, being so distinctly different from him in age, gender and role in society, still shares a mutual feeling of isolation and depression to an extent where both must turn to themselves. This connects to the global issue in that anyone can suffer from mental illness, but because their society does not acknowledge it, they are ultimately isolated and must build walls to comply with tradition.

As Clarissa attempts to conform to a generalised view on suicide, she asks again in line 19 why he had thrown himself. This rhetorical question reflects how society in this context is naturally curious about a motive for death, but because they are not familiar with mental illness, there is no existing answer. The readers then understand that Clarissa is impressed at his suicide, reflecting in lines 20 and 21 through a metaphor, conveying how she never needed to give up much in her social status to get where she is, but somehow resonated with Septimus' courage to give up practically everything he knew to follow through with his mortal decision. Lines 23 to 29 explains an extended metaphor of death being able to defy notions like the mutual experience of growing old, experiencing regret or yearning for past times. It also highlights Clarissa's admiration for him, who, in a similar position to Clarissa where they feel as if their individuality is slipping away with time, is able to refuse this through suicide. By going against suppressing views of traditionalism, Septimus maintains his 'treasure' - that is, his youth, essence of life and self-actualisation. Through this extract, Woolf conveys Clarissa's autonomy, purely by her resonation with Septimus' suicide, connecting to the global issue by discussing how self-actualisation may be achieved.

Now, moving onto 'Your Paris'; the poem as a whole was written to Hughes' late ex-wife, Sylvia Plath, who committed suicide 35 years prior to its publish. Hughes reflects on a holiday to Paris with Plath, in which he retrospectively describes and attempts to justify himself. Throughout the poem, Hughes frequently describes himself as a 'dog', attempting to 'nose' through Plath's facade which she presumably placed to divert attention from her mental health. Ultimately, he asserts that he was there for Plath's comfort when she needed it, although it was evident she was not able to express this properly; this will be elaborated on in the 40-line extract. Here, Hughes connects to the global issue by highlighting the walls placed up by those with mental illness, which has the ability to suppress introspection when others cannot help them.

Hughes continues to reference the negativity of post-war Paris throughout the poem and simultaneously criticises Plath's assumed perception of a bohemian, pre-war Paris, further emphasising how greatly Hughes may have misunderstood Plath. Consequently, it represents early cracks in their relationship, of which Plath's deceptive front would have contributed greatly to. However, it also highlights how the actions of others witnessing the facade plays a major role in influencing the self-actualisation of the victim; had Hughes done more to address Plath's approach to her world, Hughes may have at least understood her better and guided her away from her fatal end.

The extract comes from the point in the poem where Hughes reflects on Plath's mentality during the trip, describing what she may have been hiding behind her emotional walls. Again, in lines 1 and 2, Hughes refers to himself as a 'dog' using this extended metaphor, whose senses have been *'scorched'* by the *'diesel'* of Plath's ecstasies of being in an imagined Paris, revealing his eventual desensitisation to her outbursts. This contributes to his justification of his actions, where he would come to a point where Plath's manic episodes would become normalised. He understands, albeit retrospectively, that these episodes *'sealed the underground, [her] hide-out,'* and *'[her] chamber, where [she] still hung waiting for [her] torturer'*. These metaphors and the anaphora emphasises the dark extent to which her demons lay, comparing her mind to something similar to a dungeon to which she never intended to show anyone. Her 'torturer' describes not only the mental illness but her overarching wound imparted by her father's memory and death. Hughes describes in lines 7 to 9, *'Those walls, raggy with posters, were your own flayed skin - stretched on your stone god.'* There are parallels shown between Hughes' perception of Paris and Plath's strained relationship with her father; in hiding her struggles with her father, she perhaps feels a shame similar to that of those post-war utility survivors, being forced to live in the city still recovering from the impacts of war. Hughes connects this notion to her behaviour: although being *'a walking wound that the air coming against kept in a fever'*, she consistently kept a language barrier with *'practiced lips'* which *'translated [her] spasms'* into *'gushy burblings'*, to which he *'decoded into [...] conjectural, hopelessly wrong meanings'*. The extensive use of metaphors from lines 11 to 17 explains how he completely misunderstood Plath as a result of her giving *'no hint[s]'* to her mental illness, although he walked *'every corner'* with his *'fingers linked in [hers]'*.

He later reamends his view of Plath's Paris, describing her paradise as unopened 'letters' to a past lover, lying alongside writings where she expressed her depressive episodes, Hughes compares this to *'a labyrinth where [she] still hurtled, scattering tears'*. This reveals Plath's inability to express her genuine emotions towards others, not only Hughes but her ex-lover, and her attempts to 'anaesthetise' herself to the pain through writing. It also connects to the global issue by reminding the readers of external methods in which mental illness may be conveyed, instead of being shared, to avoid criticism. Instead, she turned and locked herself 'in a dream', which may have been Hughes' light-hearted opinion of Plath's manic cycles, unable to 'find the exit' from 'the torment', perhaps waiting for her illness - 'the minotaur' - to take her instead. Hughes finishes, commenting on how he could only 'yawn' and 'doze' like a dog from afar, as she numbed herself, seeming as justification for his actions. This extract overall represents what witnesses of mental health must also face; because Plath has placed emotional boundaries on her illness in an attempt to be perceived normally, she was unable to receive the comfort she needed from Hughes, which ultimately led to a form of self-actualisation where she felt she direly needed to escape.

In conclusion, both texts relate well to the global issue of mental illness and effectively discuss the stigma around the topic, which often leads to the construction of emotional facade. Both

Woolf and Hughes ultimately assert that destigmatising mental health - that is, to normalise it through exploration between mutual sufferers - is key to increased introspection and finally, self-actualisation.

3. EXAMPLE THREE (36/40)

Title: 'The physical and mental impact of unrealistic beauty standards on women'

Author: Anonymous

Session: May 2023

Level: English L&L SL

English Individual Oral Script

Literary Work – The Diet, Medusa, Beautiful by Carol Ann Duffy
Non-Literary Work – You are not yourself, Just Be Yourself, Who's The Fairest of Them All by Barbara Kruger
Global Issue – The physical and mental impact of unrealistic beauty standards on women

[0 – 1:00] I'll start my individual oral by introducing the works I will be analyzing. My main literary text is The Diet by Carol Ann Duffy, and my main non-literary text is a poster by Barbara Kruger titled 'You are not yourself.' I am linking these two works to my global issue of the impact of unrealistic beauty standards on women. My initial interest stemmed from when we did the topic of Femineity in class, but I also feel a personal connection to this issue because I feel that these expectations affect my self-esteem and self-image. In our society there are many beauty standards women are expected to follow like being a certain weight, having smooth skin, having silky hair etc. Carol Ann Duffy and Barbara Kruger are both passionate feminists and they use their works as a medium to bring out this issue using literary techniques such as personification, paradoxes, idioms, metaphors, structure, diction, and images to criticize society for the harsh expectations placed on women.

[1.00 – 3.00] Starting with the literary text, The Diet is a poem from Duffy's collection called Feminine Gospels. As the name suggests, the poem is literally about the effects of extreme dieting on a woman's body and mind. The structure consists of 8 stanzas with 7 lines each. This consistent line length per stanza throughout, reflects the strict nature of the woman's diet. The last line of each stanza is always shorter than the rest which may reflect the diet process, the woman moving from starvation to binging in a constant cycle. For the rhyme structure, there are many cases of internal rhyme for example in the end of stanza one it reads, "eight stone, by the end of the month, she was skin and bone". This is used to speed up the rhythm of the poem, pushing the woman onward in her diet journey.

Carol Ann Duffy makes use of personification in the 3rd stanza where it reads "She was Anorexia's true daughter". This personification of anorexia shown by the capitalization of the word emphasizes its power. This reveals to the audience just how much Anorexia victims obsess with weight and begin to only find comfort in their deepening condition. The paradox of 'anorexia's true daughter' which contrasts motherhood to the deadly eating disorder and portrays to the reader that the effect of this disorder is so extreme that it has become a part of the character's identity.

Additionally, Duffy uses idioms to mimic the word choice the diet industry uses to trap and trick women into losing weight. The poem begins with the line "The diet worked like a dream. No sugar, salt, dairy, fat, protein, starch, or alcohol". The phrase, "which works like a dream" is an idiom used in multiple diet advertisements when encouraging women to lose weight. Advertisements have always been used to portray to women the there is a certain standard they should reach even if it is unrealistic.

Duffy also brings out the psychological effects of starvation on this woman. This can be seen in the fifth stanza which highlights the woman's metaphorical loss of control. The wind is a metaphor of her eating disorder where "she drifted away on a breeze". This represents her losing her battle with her eating disorder.

The last line of the poem reads, "inside the Fat Woman now, trying to get out.". The diction of the word 'trying' suggests to the reader that the problem is still ongoing, trying day after day to escape the horrific cycle of binging and fasting that she has fallen into. As a reader this makes me feel pitiful for the persona because they have been paced in a never-ending cycle of anguish and mental torture because of their obsession with fitting into societal perception.

[3.00 – 4.00] This leads me to the bigger body of work called 'Medusa'. This poem describes how jealously can turn a woman into a metaphorical monster and ruin their self-confidence. The idea that if women don't conform to societal standards, they are off less worth is asserted. This is illustrated in line 14, 'perfect man, Greek God, my own; but I know you'll go, betray me, stray from home'. This use of the 'rule of three' portrays Medusa's apprehension about her husband leaving her for younger, more beautiful women.

Later in line 41, Medusa says 'Wasn't I beautiful? Wasn't I fragrant and young?'. The use of rhetorical questions reflects how Medusa believed she had to fulfill the expectations of appearing beautiful and young to ensure her man isn't unfaithful. The use of the pleading tone and past tense together once again points to the low self-esteem of the narrator. The poem ends with the line "Look at me now". This line having its own stanza makes it very impactful. It is very much a double entendre as it could be taken as the persona pleading with their partner to look at them or it could be a threat as looking at Medusa would result in your death as according to mythology looking at her results in one turning into stone.

[4.00 – 5.00] Likewise, in the poem called "Beautiful", Duffy explores the lives of four prominent women in society. A core literary technique used within the construction of Beautiful is an allusion. Although not actually saying the names of these four women, Duffy alludes to key moments or ideas from their lives. For example, in the first line it reads, "The camera loved her, close-up, back-lit," This is about Marilyn Monroe who was heavily sexualized in her prime era.

In this extract from the poem, which is about Marilyn Monroe, it reads, "They filmed on, deep, dumped what they couldn't use". Firstly, the consonance across 'deep, dumped' creates a sense of oppression and furthermore, the plosive 'p' within both these words cuts through the narrative, representing the brutality Monroe experienced on a daily basis. Duffy writes that 'she couldn't die when she died'. Even after her suicide, the media continued to use her image. Marilyn Monroe had a difficult life and Duffy uses her to bring out the media's obsession with her because she was a woman who fit into most beauty standards. It shows the audience that even when women fit into beauty standards they're still not at peace, it's a situation where they always lose.

[5.00 – 7.00] While Duffy uses poems as her medium, Barbara Kruger an American conceptual artist uses visuals instead as seen in the non-literary text, called 'You are not yourself'. This piece of work was created in 1989 with the intent to show how women who become obsessed with fitting into standards begin to realize they are losing their own identity and perhaps they never had their own identity, to begin with.

For instance, in the structure, the image depicts a girl crying in front of a broken mirror. The cracked mirror symbolizes that the girl has tried to smash her appearance, likely due to being upset or unsatisfied with how she looks. This creates an overly dramatic effect, which allows Kruger to critique the pressures put on girls from a very young age, such as looking, dressing, and acting a certain way. Kruger may use this image to reference negative self-image problems in many adolescents. A mirror should reveal a true and whole representation of oneself, but this mirror is fragmented, distorting the image of the woman.

Kruger uses black, white, and red as her primary colors in all her works. In this image, the red border is associated with passion, and energy and danger which invokes a sense of urgency in the reader, and it is also oddly similar to the way in which advertisements are designed which may be her criticizing and mocking that industry that uses advertisements to portray unrealistic standards towards women. The use of black and white images within Kruger's work may connect a viewer to earlier, or outdated times in history. Kruger is trying to criticize on how the issue of societal standards placed on women is one that is timeless as it goes from an era of black and white images, around the 19th century to our current time. The contrasting black and white values also help to create atmosphere within the work through depth, which helps to build drama and tension.

To bring out the frustration of the woman towards looking a certain way she employs diction. The small size of the word "not" indicates that society attempts to trick women into believing "You Are Yourself," in other words, that individuals are responsible for their positions in life. Barbara layers the words, "You Are Not Yourself" over the image of a mirror to critique self-image and the way that mass media runs our lives by encouraging us to have a certain appearance. Through this work, she relays the message that there is no such thing as uniqueness, but rather that humans have the natural tendency to copy what we see as "in trend." The use of the pronoun "you" also has a meaning to it. It suggests that the embedded message is directed toward everyone who views the piece. By layering this message on top of an image of a girl looking at herself, Kruger brings the viewer into a state of self-realization.

[7.00 – 8.00] A similar message is shown in another of Kruger's works, "Just be yourself". Diction is utilized in the way the picture mocks how the makeup and beauty industry use the cliché phrase, "just be yourself", while simultaneously encouraging women to look a certain way. Kruger dwells on the theme of gender roles within society and explores how women are casually subjected to achieving a concept of female perfection - namely through their facial features or physical structure. The structure of the poster showcases a heavily edited photo of a woman who has been meticulously styled paired with the caption 'You are not yourself. The irony about this is the fact that the image is encouraging their audience to stay '100%'

natural while using a woman who fits into the Eurocentric standards of being white and having blonde hair. The 100% natural mimics how when industries and celebrities act towards young impressionable women it increases their self-hatred and guilt.

[8.00 - 9.00] Subsequently, in the poster, 'Who's the fairest of them all', the colors of the photo are primarily black and white with the exception of the red boxes with the message inside. The black and white background make the writing pop and appear more dramatic. The red that the words are enclosed in may portray anger. This is the anger that most feel when they do not fit the beauty standard in this case of being fair but seeing other women who do. They end up comparing themselves to other women and their mental health gets affected as a result. Diction is used to show how beauty standards create unnecessary tension and resentment among women. There is a superlative in the phrase 'the fairest'. Creators use superlatives when they want to stress an adjective to the extreme. Barbara Kruger uses it to make it clear the woman in the picture is basing her value on whether she looks better than other women. She is bringing out how women curate their own self value and worth based on how much they fit into the societal standards compared to other women.

[9.00 - 10.00] This leads me to the conclusion of my individual oral. I'd like to argue that both the literary and non-literary works show how when women must conform to standards placed upon them, they're many negative effects that they are confronted with. These include disordered eating habits, insecurities, negative body image perceptions, flawed mental health, and loss of identity. In Duffy's poem, she talks about how the character developed an eating disorder that affected her physically and mentally, and in Barbara Kruger's poster, the woman felt as if she had lost her identity. So, to be brief, I feel as if I have adequately explored the different ways in which the global issue manifests in our society using different forms of literature. Thank you.

4. EXAMPLE FOUR (34/40)

Title: 'Gender stereotypes and portrayal of women in children's tales.'

Author: Lea Nguyen

Session: May 2023

Level: English A HL

Student: My Global Issue is gender stereotypes and the portrayal of women in children's tales. Often in children's tales women are subjected to gender stereotypes such as being weak, innocent and associated with doing housework and caregiving duties. With the rise of feminism it is important to assess the impact of the media's portrayal of gender roles, specifically on young children as they are an impressionable age group who are susceptible to the inaccurate portrayal often present in these tales. This is important as these tales shape the views of the coming generations and reinforce outdated ideals.

The extracts that I will discuss are Carol Ann Duffy's Little Red Duffy from her 1999 collection The World's Wife and Snow White, the 1937 Disney movie from 1 hour 9 minutes to 1 hour 15 minutes. While both texts contain aspects of the Global Issue, the issue is treated very differently within the texts. One embodies the stereotypes and the other challenges and tries to break them. The difference in treatment is also evident in the form of both texts and is related to the context of the time in which they were released. This commentary will analyse how women are represented in a classic children's tale which is notorious for adopting gender stereotypes as compared to a modern feminist poem and how authorial choices and style are used to convey their portrayal.

The first text I will look at is Snow White. Created with the purpose of entertainment, Snow White carries many gender stereotypes which are reinforced in society due to the film and other films like it. The scene I'll be focusing on is when Snow White meets the evil queen at the cottage in the woods. In this scene we can see that Snow White is the embodiment of gender stereotypes, specifically the ones who portray women as innocent and naive figures who require the protection of men. At the beginning of the scene we can see Snow White is making a pie while the dwarves are away at work when she's approached by the evil queen. Right from the start, the producers start with Snow White baking a pie rather than doing something recreational like relaxing or reading. This instils the idea that women should be in the kitchen cooking and preparing meals for the men who are at work. This is reflective of society's expectations of women at the time and is a stereotype that is still present today. At the beginning of the encounter the queen says 'all alone my pet?' The use of the word pet here sets the dynamic of the relationship and suggests a sense of inferiority as pet connotes submissiveness and passiveness. Additionally saying my pet asserts a sense of ownership and dominance over Snow White and in doing this the producer portrays a subservient nature which is reflective of the expectations of women at the time as it alludes to the stereotype where women are expected to be compliant to the males in their relationship, as well as the stereotype in which women are viewed as not having their own or separate identities but are defined by their relationships often to a man. Snow White's naive nature is further emphasised when she invites the evil queen, a stranger, into her house and accepts the magic apple showing gullibility and incredulity. The producers' choice for Snow White to be so unaware despite being warned by the dwarves shows ignorance and plays into the stereotypes where women are viewed as meek and naive. Because of this the dwarves have to come to Snow White's rescue, painting an image of a damsel in distress, showing impotence and a lack of independence. Furthermore as the dwarves are male characters this further emphasises that women require the protection and help of men. Additionally, the wish that she uses for her magic apple shows a lack of ambition and demonstrates the pre-existing notions about women at the time. The producers' choice for Snow White is that she wishes that the prince will carry her away to his castle and they will live happily ever after represents the passivity and the misogynistic dynamic in male and female relationships at the time and sets up the inaccurate portrayal of relationships to young children. Other parts of the film which carry stereotypes are the first scene in which Snow White is referred to as the 'lovely little princess', and when she is called the lovely maid by the magic mirror. The use of the word lovely connotes graciousness and softness and paints an image of something fragile and harmless to the audience and this reinforces outdated ideals as it sets a precedent for young girls as they believe this is how they should be. Additionally, stereotypes are portrayed through the evil queen, who's portrayed to be vain and obsessed with beauty. This reflected women at the time as they were always very conscious of their appearance because they were constantly told that their appearance was linked to their value. Additionally the queen is portrayed to be wicked and guileful and this is a common stereotype for women in literature in characters such as Lady Macbeth or Medusa who were thought to be out of character because they were not passive and took control. The stereotypes are also discussed in Little Red Cap by Carol Ann Duffy, however the representation of women is very different. In Little Red Cap, Duffy adds a twist to the children's story Little Red Riding Hood to give the female character a voice and perspective while challenging the audience to accept female sexuality. Through an autobiographical account of her relationship with an older writer, Duffy demonstrates the social bonds between men and women and breaks the stereotype of innocence and naivety. Throughout the poem Duffy feigns innocence and takes on a naive persona to mock the stereotype. The first example of this is when she uses a direct quote from Little Red Riding Hood in lines 9 and 10. In the original story it was the scene in which Little Red Riding Hood was too foolish and Duffy uses this shared knowledge to play on the naivety that is expected of women. However this naivety is juxtaposed and the stereotype is broken in lines 11 and 12. Duffy writes 'I made quite sure he spotted me', showing us that the character is taking control and thus not in a passive way, expressing a sense of wittiness that is unexpected from a female character. By making herself available so as to seduce the wolf, Little Red Cap is a sexual predator in this scene and thus is not naive or innocent. This is also ironic as even though she's a sexual predator the wolf is by nature a predator itself and there's a conflict there. Additionally the commas used in these lines quickens the pace of the poem and shows the danger felt by Little Red Cap in the seduction; she's exploring unknown territory with her sexuality. However, the commas are also used to list the different nicknames to show women such as 'babe' and 'waif' and shows that Little Red Cap knows how a young girl like her and her so-called purity is viewed by society. She uses this innocence to seduce the wolf. Duffy again resumes a passive role in the third stanza in lines 16-18. The use of the semantic field of 'crawled, ripped, snagged and murdered' uses violent imagery that suggests something is being done to the character out of her control, which is passive. The use of the world crawled creates a sense of helplessness and vulnerability as it alludes to children who are seen as unable to protect themselves and are vulnerable, adding to the passivity. The sense of incoming danger that is created by the ominous tone of these lines shows the inferiority that is felt by Little Red Cap with the wolf, even though she was the sexual predator at the beginning of the scene and this is reflective of the dynamic in modern female and male relationships as in society women are still viewed as more as inferior to men. In the fourth stanza, Duffy further shatters the stereotype of naivety and innocence and exposes the reality of female sexuality in lines 20 and 21. The use of intense sexual imagery and the exploration of female sexuality is uncommon and unexpected by female characters as women are stereotypically naive and chaste. In doing this, Duffy normalises female sexuality and draws attention to the fact that women are not as naive and innocent as they are made out to be. Duffy uses children's stories elsewhere to discuss the expectations of women, for example in Medus which is a mythological character through which Duffy highlights the expectations of women to maintain their beauty and the pressure exerted by society that women are somehow less valuable if they don't adhere to societal standards. Additionally, another poem is Salome, a Biblical character, where Duffy challenges the stereotype of women to be virtuous and demure. Instead, Salome is a cynical, wild and vibrant character who lives in the moment and contrasts with her Biblical character and the Biblical context of her story, which would expect her to be pure and virtuous.

While the content is crucial the form of both texts also play a large role in the meaning that is conveyed. With Snow White it's a children's tale which was created during a time when gender stereotypes were prominent and the need for equality was not yet recognised. Because of this the meaning conveyed is altered as it is a Disney story and we do not expect this story to be political and thus it may be inappropriate to judge the film for its portrayal as we know during these times these issues were not highlighted yet. Now we see that Disney is evolving to more portrayals which empower women in films such as Mulan, Moana and Brave. As for Little Red Cap, it is a feminist poem and thus it is expected to empower women and raise awareness about the inequalities between men and women in society, and it does exactly this. Additionally, the neat and orderly structure represents the maturity of Little Red Cap and shows that women can also be mature, level-headed and assertive and strong.

In conclusion, both texts demonstrate the issues of the misogynistic views about women but in essentially opposite ways. Little Red Cap shows society's skewed view of women while Snow White adopts these stereotypes and re-asserts them to the audience. Both texts show that the issue has been consistently prevalent from the 1930s to the 2000s and offer some explanation as to why it remains consistently an issue. As said by the feminist Andrea Dworkin, fairy tales

delineate the roles, interactions and values of men and women. They are childhood models and demonstrate how fairy tales affect the coming generations and society.

Teacher: Thank you, I just have a few follow up questions. At the end of Little Red Cap, can you look at how the character solves the problem of the wolf, how would you compare that with the way that Snow White solves her problem?

Student: In Little Red Cap, if we look at the way both characters solve their problems, Little Red Cap is a lot more assertive and in control, she takes an axe to the wolf and cuts him up to regain her freedom whereas for Snow White she prefers to be dependent on someone else and for her life to be defined by the prince, who is a male character. This is how they differ as Little Red Cap wants to be in control of her life while Snow White prefers to be by someone's side as opposed to by herself.

Teacher: would you say the last line of the Snow White extract, does that particularly emphasise her lack of control?

Student: Yes, it shows that she wants him to carry her away and she hopes that they'll live happily ever after, which is quite unrealistic. She could have gone to the prince herself but she prefers to be carried away and this emphasises the passivity that is portrayed through her character.

Teacher: In Little Red Cap, at the end of the second stanza, how does Duffy play with the normal stereotypes of female sexuality, in the line 'sweet sixteen, never been'. What is she doing there?

Student: I think that she is showing how women are viewed, she's showing the hierarchy in the two characters as we can see at the end he buys her a drink. Often in society this is seen as the first step in seduction and she provokes him to buy her a drink. She isn't innocent in this scene because of that but she is still playing into that societal construct of the patriarchal society. She seduces him to buy her a drink, because she's young she's using her attractiveness to lure him, which is where she's taking control.

Teacher: In terms of Snow White, to what extent are the directors repeating an old fairy tale or are they playing into and reinforcing the female stereotype you mentioned? Are they responsible for this stereotype or are they echoing what was there before?

Student: I think that they are just echoing what was there before because a lot of the main key parts of the film that portray gender stereotypes are in the original story and I feel like they have adapted this. However, the original story was a lot more gory and a lot more difficult to accept for the audience because it was gruesome so they took that story and they cut out all the really difficult-to-process parts and they kept everything else so they are mostly echoing everything else.

Teacher: Thank you very much, that is the end of the assessment.

STUDENT OUTLINE:

Thesis Statement (How do the 2 extracts deal with / treat the global issue you have chosen?):

While both Little Red Cap and Snow White present and contain aspects of the global issue, both texts treat the global issue in very different ways which are evident in their form and connected to the context of the time which they were released in. This commentary will analyse how women are represented in a classic children's movie, which are well known for adopting gender stereotypes, compared to a modern feminist poem and how authorial choices and style are used to convey their portrayal.

10 points for outline:
1. Global issue: Gender stereotypes and portrayal of women in children's tales. Context: Often, women subject to gender stereotypes...Important to assess impact of portrayal of gender roles on young.. tales shape views, reinforce outdated ideals. Extracts: LRC - 1999: The World's Wife, SW - 1937 Disney: 1hr9 - 1hr15

2. While both contain aspects of global issue, treated very differently (embodies vs challenges). Difference evident in form and context of time of release. Commentary will analyse...

3. Snow White - created with purpose of entertainment, carries gender stereotypes which are reinforced. Focus on scene: SW meets EQ at cottage in woods.

4. In scene, we can see SW is embodiment of stereotypes (portrayed innocent, naive, require help).
   - Baking pies while dwarves are away (producer's choice)
   - My pet → inferiority, connotes submissiveness, passiveness → stereotype: compliant women, defined by relationships
   - Inviting strangers into house → gullibility, ignorance, stereotype: meek +naive, saved by dwarves (men)
   - Wish on magic apple → passivity, misogynistic dynamic in relationship

5. Other parts of film with stereotypes:
   - First scene + magic mirror → graciousness, soft, fragile, harmless → sets precedent
   - Evil queen: obsessed with beauty + wicked, guileful

6. Also discussed in LRC by CAD, representation is different. Duffy adds twist to children's story to give female voice, perspective while challenging to accept female sexuality. Autobiographical recount to demonstrate imbalance + break stereotype

7. Duffy feigns innocence + takes on innocent persona to mock stereotype
    - Direct quotes from LRRH → show naivety expected
    - Juxtaposed, stereotype broken: "I made quite sure.." → takes control (not passive), expressing unexpected wittiness
        - Commas → quickens pace, shows excitement
            → list different nicknames, shows she knows how her "purity" is viewed (sexualised)
    - Resumes passive role (stanza 3), use of semantic field to create violent imagery → out of her control
        - "crawled" → allusion to child who are vulnerable.. → passive stereotype
        - Vicious tone, sense of impending danger → shows inferiority, reflective of modern dynamic
    - Shatters stereotype (4th stanza), exposes reality of female sexuality through use of sexual imagery → normalises, breaks stereotype

8. Other texts within body of work:
    Medusa - expectation of women to maintain their beauty and the pressure exerted by society that women less valuable
    Salome - Biblical character, challenge stereotype to be virtuous and demure, Salome is cynical, wild

9. The form of the texts play a large role in the meaning that is conveyed:
    SW = children's tale, audience don't expect to be political
    LRC = feminist poem, carries message, neat + order structure → maturity

10. Demonstrate issue of misogynistic view but in opposite ways. Text shows issues have been consistently prevalent (1930s-2000s) + offers explanation
    Quote: "Fairy tales are the primary information of the culture. They delineate the roles, interactions, and values which are available to us. They are our childhood models,"

5. EXAMPLE FIVE (37/40)

Title: 'The characterization of women by their possessions and status

Author: M. Clark

Session: May 2023

Level: English A SL

Individual Oral Student Outline Form

Global Issue:	The characterisation of women by their possessions and status
Texts Chosen:	
Literary Work:	Carol Ann Duffy New Selected Poems
Non-Literary Work:	Lauren Greenfield's Generation Wealth Photography

Notes for oral (maximum of 10 bullet points):

1. FOI culture+identity, discussing GI [relates to] lit+non-lit. CAD - 1st female poet laureate + feminist-evident in NSP. 1stPNar-voice to historic figs deconstructs gender stereotypes + empowers female protagonists. LG GWF, focus-influence of affluence +aspiration of wealth, greed and excess - demeans individuality + emphasises materialism

2. Lit extract - Salome(provides) perspective {dramatic monologue}. Starts with imagery(4)- double entendre. Original story+symbolism lustrous lifestyle. Head-importance of appearance-lack of body-powerless + Tag rhetoric q-blase+indirect address -many men. ^standards appearance [reinforced] (6) objectify -reverse GS - empower+differentiate.

3. [Similarly] -(15). Listing of many men+biblical allusion - undermining religion-empowerment, common name-indifference to men. (17)-conforming stereotype-above such women. [Also illustrates] sluggish (20). "Cl" [percussive consonance]-emphasis. [Furhter illustrated] (27), polysndetic listing - arduous. Modernised diction-nouns vs verb - familiarity.

4. GI explored in AH (wife) - sonnet written in iambic pentameter-mimics speech-authentic. Like husband's work -identity. Breaks sonnet-no rhyme-not confined by husband. 2nd best bed-metaphor for romance+affirmation of love-1st reserved for guests - incomprehensible. [Described as] "spinning world" of "forests, castles, cliff-tops, seas"-asyndetic list emphasis

5. [Applicable to] SWN-voice to subject of Georges Braque's painting "big nude". "Bourgeoisie" vs "river-whore" juxtaposition in status-class distinction. Art vs art-capitonym-importance of status "You're getting thin. not good"-direct address, contrast title-adjective suggests value of body to make a "few franks", hard alliteration - rough sound- accentuates harsh lifestyle

6. Open-ended approach addressing GI in LG GWF. Non-lit extract, candid image illustrating obnoxiously saturated pink labels-more vivid+pure angled at cam, social conformity. Contrasts monochromatic complementary colours of dress. Bold text-adj paid-importance. Multiple-removes individuality

7. [Composition] same effect. RO3rds for labels reinforces importance. DOF makes tags stand out-closer to cam=centre of interest. Vertically transposed frame-smaller aperture increases aspect ratio->crops out faces, taking away identity-how society views women +materialism

8. GI applicable to all ages- Toddlers and Tiaras star Eden Wood, 6 at time of photo. Clearly subject of image-negative space and vignetting-nothing to see in background. Precocious sexualisation - importance irrespective of age- deliberate focus on hair, makeup, earrings provokes uncomfort. Reinforced by high-angle shot -smaller, vulnerable as subject.

9. [Further sexualisation]-13 year old boy at west hollywood nighclub-gazing at older girl's chest. Positioned in centre+overexposure=>bokeh+chromatic aberration-less distinguishable->loss of identity. Background underexposed-involuntary focus on boy looking at chest. Horizontal line of symmetry in line with eyes and chest+3D effect from distortion - grabs attention

> 10. GI sustained for years-salome in 1st centry-> LG photos. Applies to all ages- importance of possessions+status = loss of identity. CAD poetry-use of DM, list, allit+ metaphor. Deconstruct gender stereotype-empower,authority. LG comp. exposure. DOF-centre of focus obvious. Aspect ratio strips identity-focus on materialism+beauty=identity, irrespective of age

Salome

I'd done it before
(and doubtless I'll do it again,
sooner or later)
woke up with a head on the pillow beside me – whose? –
what did it matter?
5

Good-looking, of course, dark hair, rather matted;
the reddish beard several shades lighter;
with very deep lines around the eyes,
from pain, I'd guess, maybe laughter;
and a beautiful crimson mouth that obviously knew
10
how to flatter...
which I kissed...
Colder than pewter.
Strange. What was his name? Peter?

Simon? Andrew? John? I knew I'd feel better
15
for tea, dry toast, no butter,
so rang for the maid.
And, indeed, her innocent clatter
of cups and plates,
her clearing of clutter,
20
her regional patter,
were just what I needed –
hungover and wrecked as I was from a night on the batter.

Never again!

I needed to clean up my act,
25
get fitter,
cut out the booze and the fags and the sex.
Yes. And as for the latter,
it was time to turf out the blighter,
the beater or biter,
30
who'd come like a lamb to the slaughter
to Salome's bed.

Lauren Greenfield Generation Wealth Photography

6. EXAMPLE SIX (38/40)

Title: 'How Oppression Fuels Rebellion'

Author: M. Clark

Session: May 2023

Level: English A HL

ENGLISH IO - HOW OPPRESSION FUELS REBELLION (Script)

The purpose of this oral discussion, categorized under the field of inquiry of Politics, Power, and Justice, is to examine how repression fuels rebellion. In the history of humanity, we have witnessed numerous expressions of this issue, from the Iranian Revolution in 1978, the rise of the Iranian people in a response to an oppressive regime to the existence of rebel groups that actively fight against occupation. Additionally, the issue also manifests itself inside households, as studies have demonstrated that overly-strict parenting eventually leads to more rebellious children.

The literary-work that will be used to analyze the issue is Persepolis by Marjane Satrapi, 2002, a graphic memoir and Bildungsroman narrating the coming-of-age of Marji, an Iranian girl who grows up in a revolution and war-ravaged Iran overthrown by oppressive theocratic forces. Although seemingly simple and infantile in appearance, it discusses major pressing global issues relating to the intrinsic nature of political and personal life in a context of political instability. The book portrays the complexity of growing up during the Iranian Revolution and how political and social instability shape Marji's growth, developing from a naïve character easily influenced by the government's ideals, to an independent thinker who rebels against the law and develops her own conscience.

The theme of rebellion, defined as refusing to adhere to the law or set of rules, appears throughout the novel in different forms and shapes as Marji and the rest of Iran find ways to resist the oppressive rules imposed by the Islamic Republic. This is reflected during instances in the novel through individual acts of rebellion, such as the appearance of women wearing veils the wrong way, or through Uncle Anoosh, serving as a symbol of resistance against oppression. Rebellion, in this case, is a clear indication of a defense mechanism against the restriction of freedom of expression. Furthermore, the novel additionally includes collective rebellion that appears in the shape of uprisings and protests against the authorities.

With all these manifestations of the issue, we will now focus our attention towards chapter 15, The Cigarette, which seems to be a turning point in the narrative as it depicts our global issue more explicitly. For more context, as oppression escalates in the world around Marji and the regime starts executing people with differing perspectives, Marji's mother reacts by becoming even stricter with her daughter out of fear for her life. As a response to this heightening of oppression both by her mother and by the Government, Marji takes a more active approach when it comes to rebelling. Now, I will more precisely analyze how Satrapi explicitly denounces this issue through the following authorial choices in page 117: parallelism, metaphor and symbolism.

On the four last frames of the page, Marji is portrayed as the center of the image while she takes her first cigarette with an expression of discomfort and agony, contrasting with the neutrality of the dark background. The insubordinate act of smoking symbolizes rebellion. She is burning the last remainder of her conformity, and therefore, she is rebelling. The gesture takes a broader meaning as this act is directed against all the repressions in her life: from her parents, who rightly pressure her to behave responsibly, but also from the regime, which makes life restrictive enough that she has to break the law in order to enjoy normal life. Marji says: I kissed my childhood goodbye. Now I was a grown-up. Satrapi employs the words goodbye and grown-up to conjugate with the image of the cigarettes to imply that she is saying goodbye to docility, and she is forming her own individuality. Individuality in this case is symbolized by growing up which represents independence, as a sign of rebellion to the oppression of the Government.

BOW: *Western elements are employed throughout the novel to symbolize - western values are a type of rebellion against ideology*

Satrapi employs parallelism in order to show how the repression of Marji parallels the repression of citizens, thus leading to her rebellion having a double-meaning. She uses the metaphor of (Dictator. You are the guardian of the revolution of this house) , intending that all aspects in her life are influenced by dictatorship, and therefore her need for freedom is expressed through her rebellion against her mothers oppression which is caused by the Government's repression. In Persepolis, we can see that personal and political life are inexorably intertwined, as the Islamic Regime dictates the moral code of society. In this case, to assert one's individuality in clothing or spoken opinion becomes a political act. Marjane uses the language of the regime—"dictatorship"—to describe her relationship with her mother indicates just how intertwined her personal life has become with the larger political issues of her day.

BOW: - she gets attacked by women due to outfit choice

For the non-literary text, I have selected to analyze Mass Niessens photographs. This photographer generally focuses on contemporary social issues such as inequality and human rights violations. In a single click he can immortalize a significant political issue forever for all humanity to see. What is particular about him, is that he himself employs his art, photography, as a tool for rebellion against oppression. For instance, in 2015, he was the winner of the Word Press Photography Contest with an image that represented a gay Russian couple, which was seen as a symbol of rebellion against the oppressive homophobic policies of the Russian Government

However, today, the image that I have chosen to analyze depicts the Libyan Revolution. For brief context, it was set during the Libyan Revolution of 2011, which consisted of a collective rebellion of the Libyan people as a response to Muammar Gaddafi's 40-year-long oppressive dictatorship. The photography explicitly conveys the global issue of how oppression fuels rebellion through the use of symbolism, imagery and pathos that are depicted through three key elements: the flag, the man and the burning tank.

Through all the 9 pictures from Niessens Libya's collection, the flag is a recurrent symbol used to appeal to the Libyans national identity. In this image specifically, the man standing is holding a Libyan flag from the pre-Gaddafi days. Through the use of this old flag, the author appeals to the pathos of the Libyans, as it makes them reminiscent of the pre-dictatorship era. The aim of the creation of this nostalgia serves to incite the rest of the population to rebel against oppression in order to recover the freedom that existed before Ghaddafis rule. Additionally, it also serves a political statement due to the fact that it goes against the convictions of the regime, and therefore can be considered as a type of rebellion in itself as it is infringing the set rules.

BOW: The flag comes up quite often - in the child it is the main focus of the image - his work in general is characterized by the use of pathos.

The second element that will be analyzed is the use of imagery in order to portray this rebellion against repression. The effect is achieved through the positioning of the man, as he is standing and is positioned in the top part of the image. The man himself is a symbol of the Libyan population as he is the main focus of the image and he holds the Libyan flag that serves to unite the whole population under a national symbol. The fact that he is standing, which must be highlighted, in this case, symbolizes the rise of the population. The population rises against the regime, which itself is a type of rebellion against oppression.

BOW: As a professional photographer he uses his technical knowledge to better convey the messages, mathematical devices, symmetry, tricks to attract the attention of the audience in order to share a specific message

The last device that will be analyzed is a portrayal of a burning tank. Through this event, the author conveys the idea of the destruction of the Libyans society conformity to oppression. In this case, we can create a parallel with the symbol of cigarettes in Persepolis, as the burning indicates a destruction of conformity, and therefore an act of rebellion. While in Persepolis Marji's act is an individual act of rebellion, in this image this act is collective as it is taken by all the population through protests. In this case, the tank acts as a symbol for the military power which Ghaddafi employed in order to restrict his population - indeed, he used hard power to oppress the society through the use of threats and fear, which instead of conformity only lead to rebellion as seen on the image.

7. EXAMPLE SEVEN (37/40)

Title: 'The reluctance to have conversations about death in society'

Author: Anonymous

Session: May 2023

Level: English Lang & Lit HL

Good afternoon, this is my individual oral for the academic year 2022-2023. My oral will be focusing on the Global Issue of the reluctance to have conversations about death in society. These severe conversations are still not prevalent today because of them still being considered taboo to discuss. I will be exploring this global issue through the literary text Holy Sonnet 10 by John Donne from the poem collection Metaphysical Poetry and the non-literary ad campaign titled "Whatever You Call It" by the Terminal Illness Charity foundation called Marie Curie.

The idea that death is unknowable and inevitable is something that scares us, and it's as if talking about it forces us to face this reality. This is exactly what scares people away from talking about death, but the works I have chosen show a contrasting view to this issue and encourage people to face this issue head-on. From the use of personification, synecdoches, and a derisive tone in the literary work and the use of euphemisms, personification and colour psychology in the non-literary work, the creators of these texts aim to encourage people to not be afraid of having conversations about death and bringing it mainstream.

I will be first talking about my literary work. The poem is an addressal to death, and it works to demerit the power of death on human lives. Donne uses a triumphant and (at times) mocking tone to reinforce the idea that death is not something to fear, but is rather an intermediary between life and eternal solitude.

The poem characterises death as vain and prideful from the first line.
The speaker expresses his opposition to death being viewed as a powerful, authoritative figure. He essentially argues that no one who dies is truly dead. Despite the fact that death is presented as a pompous figure who happily plays on its reputation as "mighty and dreadful," the speaker utilizes logical argument to personify death as petty and impotent.

To present "poor death" as a pitiful character, the speaker addresses death directly, arguing that "not yet canst thou murder me," and rapidly establishing the poem as a message of defiance. Moreover, in line 8, death is represented as a pathway between life on earth and the afterlife, a period in which one can "rest their bones" and wake to a sweet eternity after death, where sleep is used as a conventional analogy for death. Bones here are a synecdoche for the physical body left behind and separated from the soul when someone dies.

Sleep is considered a period of rejuvenation, so death's prideful nature about humans being afraid of death holds no ground. Using this analogy also makes death seem like a peaceful end, so the reader is not fearful of its implications. This supports the idea that death is a natural part of the human life cycle and talking about it should not be an inhibition. To add insult to injury, the speaker goes on to mention that poppy—perhaps referring to opiates— and charms do more to bring rest to one's life than sleep (or in this case death) does, hence death is always inferior to something either way, so there is nothing to be prideful about.

Death is also shown in the poem as a "slave" to earthly things, highlighting it's frailty. The speaker suggests that "Fate, chance, kings... desperate men... poison, war, and sickness" are all things that come to mind while thinking of death. Its life is entirely reliant on earthly objects like these. Furthermore, these figures cannot be controlled by death due to their unpredictable nature. Death is thus a slave rather than a lord of anything. On the contrary, Henry Vaughan portrays death as a glorified object of desire in his poem 'They are all gone into the world of light'. This serves the same purpose of mainstreaming the idea of death in society but does this in a contrasting manner to Donne.

The use of anaphora with the word 'and' in lines 10-12 serve to appeal to the emotions of the reader and emphasise on the powerlessness of death. The global issue is highlighted through the poet's stance on this issue. He tells the reader to be unafraid of death and reassures them about the bliss they will achieve after death.

The last line is a seemingly self-contradictory phrase, a paradox. How can death, in any case, die? Death, and especially life after death, is an ambiguous topic. As a result, the speaker employs the contradiction of "Death, thou shall die" as a last claim of triumph through the implication of the immortal soul. Donne has thus succeeded in defeating the idea of death being an ominous figure here to claim the lives of our loved ones.

I will now discuss how my non-literary text exemplifies the global issue. Phrases like 'kick the bucket', 'take your last bow' and 'cash in your chips' are euphemisms used by society to avoid saying the 'd-word' and make it sound less offensive. Through this ad campaign, the foundation aimed at encouraging people to start having these conversations about death and planning for the inevitable.

All the ads are similarly structured: a euphemism about death is emboldened on half the page and the rest is a visual representation of this euphemism through simple animations. This allows the ads to seem more lighthearted when compared to what they are actually meant to euphamize. This already sets the tone for the advertisement before the viewer has a chance to process the intentions behind it. The bucket with the googly eyes is being personified, as if to represent someone literally 'kicking the bucket'. This may seem quite insensitive on the surface but is a suitable way of doing exactly what the euphemism is intended to do. It brings a sense of lightheartedness to a topic that is heavy and ominous. This sets a casual tone to the ad and thus it's message can be read in such a fashion by the viewer too. Moreover, the word death never seems to appear on these advertisements. I believe that this is done intentionally to highlight the fact that society never talks about death.

The colour palette used for the ad is very striking. The red-green pastel contrast is one that traditionally exists in the opponent process colour model, that is colours that don't usually complement each other. The Take Your Last Bow ad employs this colour scheme as well with the blue-yellow combination. This palette represents the stark difference between the text and the animation and separating the two makes them easily readable and eye-catching.

The animations themselves are not meant to look-realistic. Making them look realistic would not allow the creators to achieve the aspect of lightening the tone of the advertisement. This is because when they look unrealistic rather than lifelike, the viewers do not associate the message behind the advertisement directly to their lives. This advertisement can be associated to the rising crest before the dip into the uncanny valley, where the purposeful decrease in realism bypasses the viewer's increase in discomfort, allowing the message to be delivered in an effortless manner.

The ads were compiled into a video made by the foundation with a nursery-rhyme like tune playing in the background. This further throws out the aspect of the seriousness of a topic like death— one that is especially heinous to mention in a nursery rhyme for children— and makes such an issue seem like an everyday conversation to be had. The instrumental is catchy, and sticks with the viewer even after having watched the ad. This along with the bright colours allow the video to not be disregarded by the viewer even after having watching it, allowing it's message to linger.

The visual path of the viewer flows in a sequential manner from the euphemism, to the animation to the small message at the bottom of the page, which is perhaps the most impactful. "Whatever you call it, we should talk about it" directly addresses this stigma against having conversations about death. The use of 'we' is important in this line. It promotes a sense of shared responsibility and doesn't put the onus on the viewer to implement on their own. The imperative 'should' is used to show obligation and to recommend the viewer to have conversations about death with the people around them, while not sounding like a stern order at the same time due to its playful nature.

Death has always been a taboo topic in society, one that is off-limits to talk about. This makes loss after death seem even harder to cope up with, as it came as a shock rather than something they were prepared for. This makes it all the more important to have these conversations and be prepared for death when the time comes, so they may handle it better. The metaphysical poets and the Marie Curie foundation thus, through the usage of literary and advertising techniques, promote the need to have conversations about death in society and to not be fearful of its consequences.

8. EXAMPLE EIGHT (36/40)

Title: 'The significance of memory in shaping the identities of individuals'

Author: Anonymous

Session: May 2023

Level: English A Lit SL

IO Outline – Zoom in and then zoom out

IO Prompt: *Examine the ways in which the global issue of your choice is presented through the content and form of the two works that you have studied.*

Narrowed Down Global Issue:
The significance of memory in shaping the identities of individuals

---

1-minute introduction:
Today, in my individual oral, I am going to explore the field of inquiry, culture, identity and community. More specifically, I'd like to discuss the global issue of the significance of memory in shaping the identities of individuals, and how that specifically can affect the way that they can recover after experiencing a major traumatic event.

2-minute extract discussion (work in language A) zooming in on specific and detailed examples of the author's choices in connection to the global issue:

Main claim/argument for this portion of the IO: After all that Kambili has gone through at the hands of her father, she still managed to find her voice/identity and rise up from the pain. However, the memories of her father and what he preached still weigh her down, resulting in a sort of hybrid identity between this new empowered Kambili, and the younger Kambili that still yearns for her father's affection.

Piece(s) of evidence to support the claim/argument:
1. "Silence hangs over us, but it is a different kind of silence, one that lets me breathe"
2. "I have not told Jaja that I offer Masses for Papa every Sunday, that I want to see him in my dreams, that I want it so much I sometimes make my own dreams, when I am neither sleep nor awake: I see Papa, he reaches out to hug me.."
3. "There is so much that is still silent between Jaja and me. Perhaps we will talk more with time, or perhaps we never will be able to say it all, to clothes things in words, things that have long been naked"
4. "I can talk about the future now"
5. "We'll plant nee orange trees in Abba when we come back, and Jaja will plant purple hibiscus, too, and I'll plant ixora so we can suck the juices of the flowers"
6. "The new rains will come down soon"
7. "Jaja's defiance seemed ... like Aunty Ifeoma's experimental purple hibiscus: rare, fragrant with the undertones of freedom."

Unpacking of the evidence - Name the formal or technical choice(s) in your evidence and add your analysis and interpretation of how meaning is created:

1. Nature symbolism- nature is often used to symbolise both peace and freedom, it represents the cycle that we undergo throughout life, and is something that is deeply rooted in our past. In this extract, Adichie uses this nature symbolism to highlight how the characters are moving on and letting go of the heavy memories of the past that hold them back, it is them saying that no, this will not shape who we are.
    a. Plants: A symbol of peace, the idea that they will plant something lasting and watch it grow hint at the new serenity they've found, connects to what Kambili says, "I can talk about the future now"
    b. Rain: This novel is concluded with one short line "The new rains will come down soon", which serves as a symbol for a fresh start and a new hope, a sort of cleansing that the characters will experience.
    c.
2. Motif of Silence- The metaphor of silence hanging over the family is presented early on in this extract, where Kambili compares the silence that they're experiencing right now to the stifling one that hung over them when they were under the mercy of Papa.
    a. Metaphors - silence is said to be a naked thing, connotations of vulnerability and meekness. Silence = lack of freedom
3. Juxtaposition of peace/conflict - Through this juxtaposition, Adichie urges us to take a closer look at Kambili. While at first glance it may seem like Kambili has recovered from papa's death, and has found her voice after 15 (or more) years of blindly following after her father ("one that lets me breathe"), the nightmares that she is experiencing hint to a deeper internal conflict. The memory of her father still haunts her. Her identity is still a melding of the empowered young woman who found her confidence and the little girl that still desperately yearns for and seeks her father's approval.
    a. Nightmares

2-minute whole work discussion (work in language A) zooming out on larger authorial choices in connection to the global issue.

Main claim/argument for this portion of the IO:
Some aspects of this issue can also be seen throughout the novel as a whole. Kambili is often struggling with dissociating from her father's ideals, and holds on tightly to his memory whenever she is confronted with something new.

Piece(s) of evidence to support the claim/argument:
1. "I meant to say I am sorry Papa broke your figurines, but the words that came out were, I'm sorry your figurines broke, Mama."

2. "Because Papa-Nnukwu is a pagan." Papa would be proud that I had said that."
3. "Because Nsukka could free something deep inside your belly that would rise up to your throat and come out as a freedom song, as laughter."
4. "I no longer wonder if I have a right to love Father Amadi; I simply go ahead and love him"

Unpacking of the evidence - Name the formal or technical choice(s) in your evidence and add your analysis and interpretation of how meaning is created:

1. Kambili refers to Papas beliefs and values wherever confronted with the unknown, and tries her hardest to please him, to be the perfect daughter that he built up. This shows when she succumbs to the silence that holds her prisoner. When she doesn't admit that Papa broke mama's figurines, or when she calls Papa-Nnukwu a pagan, the only thing in her mind is that she is making Papa proud - this is something that the kambili we see in the extract still struggles with. She sees her father in her nightmares, and wants to reach out and hug him, to be consoled and told that she has made him proud (maybe also the reason why she still offers Masses for him every Sunday)
    a. Juxtaposition is again used, nightmares and laughter to accentuate the fact that no matter how hard she tries, a Part of Papa has already left an impression on her, and like it or not his memory will stay with her - it is now a part of her identity.
2. Also seen as a whole throughout the novel , as we are introduced to the titular purple hibiscuses, and are told that their unique colour is a result of an experiment done by one of Aunty Ifeoma's friends. Jaja tends to the flowers in Nsukka, and brings some back with him when they go back home. Throughout the novel, those purple hibiscuses have come to represent the freedom that both Kambili and Jaja begin to discover in Nsukka, away from Papa's authoritative hold. The flowers are unusual in their colour, but yet boast it confidently and are considered beautiful.

2-minute extract discussion (work in translation) zooming in on specific and detailed examples of the author's choices in connection to the global issue:

Main claim/argument for this portion of the IO:
A moral internal conflict affecting the whole community, even years after Santiago's death. Both memory of the murder, and the guilt associated with it hang over the people of the town, shaping them into who they are (identity) years later.

Piece(s) of evidence to support the claim/argument:
1. "For years we couldn't talk about anything else. Our daily conduct, dominated then by so many linear habits, had suddenly begun to spin around a single common anxiety"

2. "...none of us could go on living without an exact knowledge of the place and the mission assigned to us by fate"
3. "Two bloody knives that weren't bloody yet"
4. "Don Rogelio... marvel of vitality... got up for the last time..."
5. "Twelve days after the crime, the investigating magistrate came upon a town that was an open wound."
6. "He had to ask for troop reinforcements to control the crowd that was pouring in to testify without having been summoned, everyone eager to show off their own important role in the drama."
7. "On the other hand, she never forgave herself for having mixed up the magnificent augury of trees with the unlucky one of birds, and she succumbed to the pernicious habit of her time of chewing pepper cress seeds."

Unpacking of the evidence - Name the formal or technical choice(s) in your evidence and add your analysis and interpretation of how meaning is created:

1. **Tone of narration (clinical and journalistic)** - placid, detached, objective = crucial in giving us a good account... yet even with all this we are never too sure. Is the narrator reliable, or did his memories of the murder shape his who he is now? He includes himself in the "none of us" - which means that intrinsically he considers himself guilty as well.
    a. How is this achieved? Clinical descriptions ("two bloody knives that weren't bloody yet")
    b. Why? Unreliability of memory and contradicting witness accounts (subjective) - try to lend more credibility to the story but in the end the narrator still fails as we are left with many questions
    c. Guilt is clearly stated several types
2. **Irony** - the death was foretold, everyone knew that it was about to take place, yet through accident, choice, laziness, or rationalisation no one tries to prevent the killing. This in-action/silence can be viewed as a form of acceptance. No one does anything to stop it.
    a. One person that's not really guilty is the only one that carries the guilt - unhealthy way though, since absolution is unattainable, Plácida obsesses over the past instead.
    b. Metaphor ("open wound") - no matter how much they try to absolve themselves of the guilt, it still haunts them
3. **Magical realism (theme of fate)** - throughout this chapter, allusions to fate are made, this is because the inevitability of Santiago's death plays a fundamental role in the townspeople's willingness to let go of the guilt that hangs over them, and continue living their lives normally. Despite that though - they aren't able to do just that, and many of them suffer fatal and tragic consequences, like Hortensia Baute who went mad.

> a. The fact that everyone's memories were so muddled, and made it impossible to arrive at any semblance of truth about the incident can also be considered a fated matter.
> b. how blaming powers outside of our control is more comforting than confronting the truth. - using memory as justification (i.e. memory of the cause, honour)

2-minute whole work discussion (work in translation) zooming in on specific and detailed examples of the author's choices in connection to the global issue:

Main claim/argument for this portion of the IO:
The murder of Santaigo Nasar was a majorly traumatic event that clearly (and severely) affected the whole town. Remnants of the day of the murder can be seen in the current identiies of the inhabitants of the twon in the form of memories. Case in point, the novel is written so many years after the event, and yet most people still remember it (albeit not very clearly)

Piece(s) of evidence to support the claim/argument:
1. "Many people coincided in the recalling that it was a radiant morning with a sea breeze coming in through the banana groves, as was to be expected in a fine February of that period. But most agreed that the weather was funeral, with a cloudy, low sky and the thick smell of still waters, and that at the moment of the misfortune a thin drizzle like the one Santiago Nasar had seen in his dream grove was falling."
2. "I returned to this forgotten village, trying to put the broken mirror of memory back together from so many scattered shards"
3. " I decided to rescue it piece by piece from the memory of others"
4. "Not just me. Everything continued to smell of Santiago Nasar that day. The vicario brothers could smell him in the jail cell where the mayor had locked them up; he could think of something to do with them. "No matter how much I scrubbed with soap and rags I couldn't get rid of the smell," Pedro Vicario told me.

Unpacking of the evidence - Name the formal or technical choice(s) in your evidence and add your analysis and interpretation of how meaning is created:
1. Motif/imagery of smell - smell is a recurring motif in the novel, especially towards the end as many of the townspeople mention how everything reeked of Santaigo Nasar following the murder. Smell is the sense most closely associated with memory, so it is likely that this is their memory of the event highlighting the guilt that they felt at the time (that's why everyone is in agreement about the smell, but not say the weather).

> a. The scent of Santiago in a way drives the brothers crazy, although it is likely that this scent only exists in their minds, and is perpetuated by their guilt.
> 2. Fragmented memory (trying to forget the guilt they carry from that day.)
>   a. Weather accounts, inaccuracies in descriptions due to hazy recollection - or lies?
>   b. Imagery to underscore this idea of fragmented memory, e.g. broken mirror.
>
> Therefore... the memory of Santiago's death haunts everyone in the town, forever changing who they are.

1-minute conclusion/synthesis:
Return to the global issue at hand. Why does it matter?
Return to the techniques and choices used by both authors in the extract and the body of work or whole work. How is the global issue presented in both the work and the text? Why? Make sure this isn't just a list of devices or features!
Try to synthesise what both authors have done in connection to the global issue. What's interesting or insightful about the ways in which they have explored the global issue?
If you want to do so, go abroad. Why does all of this matter? How might this connect to TOK? What makes this worth studying?

9. EXAMPLE NINE (35/40)

Title: 'The sexualization of girlhood by society'

Author: Anonymous

Session: May 2023

Level: English A Lang and Lit HL

In my IO, I will be analyzing the global issue of the sexualization of girlhood by society. I find this particularly striking because we see sexist things on a day to day basis, and we realize when we are already into our teenage years, that we have been living through this since childhood. I decided to bring together the work of Duffy and Donnelly, two admirable and clear sighted women that know exactly how to use the power of words and images with the purpose of portraying the issues of the world. Carol Ann Duffy's poem, little red cap, together with Liza Donnelly's iconic "good girl or slut" cartoon, show the harsh reality of today's world. With the poem being published in 1999, and the cartoon published in 2011, there is more than a decade in between. The situation hasn't changed, and these women use their voice to protest against it. Carol Ann Duffy explores the global issue of the sexualization of girlhood through her use of narrative poetry and symbolism.

Her work is open to interpretation. This poem is part of a poetry anthology called the world's wife made up of 30 poems written in dramatic monologue that balance the essence of the past and the thoughts of the contemporary, putting a new perspective on patriarchal stories.

In this particular poem she clearly narrates a sexist story. There is a semantic field of naivety, and one of danger. A semantic field of childhood, and one of violence. Together, it tells the main character's journey. The early reversion back to the fairytale language in a reference to the original story shows that there is still an element of childhood present. Even if she is at the legal age of consent, barely, that doesn't mean to be emotionally ready.

And then she makes sure she's spotted. This makes the reader question. Why does she? Was this expected? And if so, from whom? She might just want this to feel like she's in control, to feel like she's a big girl now, not fitting into the stereotypes of a "good girl". This line of thought connects with my analysis of the cartoon later on.

Further into the second verse, she states she's just sixteen. She feels like she is older than her age but the truth is she is very inexperienced. He bought her her first drink. How was she to know how vulnerable she would become.

And then she feels the need to explain herself. To justify herself. She thinks she's defying the system by taking control. When in reality the wolf was always in control, knowing how to take advantage of the situation and of the girl.

At some point, she's come too far to back out. It might even be dangerous to change her mind now.

And then there is scarring sex. Her stockings ripped. Her blazer snagged.

"But got there." Those three words are the most important ones in the poem. It sounds like she was just trying to reach a goal, to check something off her list. Got where? Sexual maturity, maybe. The way she says it sounds as though she had a destination, probably set by society itself, and she completed it. More like something she felt she had to do, to break out of a cycle, or to complete it.

She probably grew up being sexualized, and so guessing something like this is the way things happen.

The pace is increased in this verse, with no conjunctions, like everything is happening too fast for her to control any more.

But then she was young. Yes. young and naïve, young and sexualized. Young… and didn't know better. So she ended up trapped in patriarchy. It took her ten years to realize that being free also meant not being sexualized, it meant she always had the choice. She didn't have to want it.

And then, just then. She realized.

Moving on to the symbolism in the poem, his verse, his paperback. It's almost a script-like flirtation method to 'seduce' all or multiple women. Like he's done it a million times before. There is also the whole symbolism surrounding the wolf. The word "HE", nameless. Allegorical. One that represents many. He has a bad boy vibe. Intimidating and sexy. The patriarchal, dominant, and dangerous male predator is still present.

Going further, the forest represents her lack of knowledge of what would truly come next. Her blazer, a school girl. And clothes are suggestions that her innocence is being torn away and signs of violence. Then two harsh phrases. "Murder clues" and "I lost both shoes". Murder clues mean that despite feeling like she's leading, like she's in control, the wolf had planned every step, he had the real advantage the whole time. The shoes represent losing her virginity. To some extent, she feels like what happened was her fault. She lost both shoes. She thinks maybe she asked for it. When the truth is she would have been sexualized regardless of her actions.

Again, ten years later, she put it all together. It took her ten years to realize that it was never her fault. And she says, "A mushroom stoppers the mouth of a buried corpse" This line connects directly to my global issue. The buried corpse is the little girl, girlhood, childhood. And the mushroom is sexualization. So she finally realized that sexualization at such an early age is what abruptly cut her now-buried childhood short.

It's dark, but it puts things into perspective. Now, like Duffy, Donnelly's work has many different ways it can be interpreted. Today I will look at one of her most famous cartoons, the "good girl or slut".

In this cartoon, Donnelly presents the global issue of the sexualization of girlhood through her use of taboo language in striking ways. When your eyes scan the cartoon for the first time, the word 'slut' jumps out at you. It's the shock factor. The issue here is clear. When a child talks about what they want to be when they grow up, words like lawyer, doctor, pilot come up. Not slut. Girls act based on what society thinks, and they are labelled for the way they act, and the labels are made by society, and this just goes on forever. Isn't it ironic how it all comes full circle? The statement is taboo for many reasons. Either girls are "good" (with all the sexual implications that come with the word "good" in this context) - a term that, when referring to girls, is defined by men - and if they are any less than "good", they are sluts. In fact, based on the dolls' clothes, it is implied that sometimes a girl is not even labelled for her behaviour, but for the way they dress, and this is true at any age, this example of sexualization is seen every day in school dress-codes. This is all part of a criteria. A criteria built by men and enforced by both men and women since forever. Instead of living a spontaneous and free life, we are trapped, thinking twice, three times, before we act. Our every move can easily become the centre of attention, become sexualized. Even as girls are growing up, there is a standard set of rules we know about, normal things we factor into our day to day decisions that boys never think about. The word slut used by girls that young is a problem, but so is any other taboo word. The issue with this one is the fact that these little girls actually thought about it. There is also the fact that it is girlhood that is sexualized. Not childhood. Two little boys would never be having this conversation. There is not even a male equivalent of slut. Taking into account that the word "man-whore" implies that the word "whore" is meant for females in the first place. And that the words "player" or "fuckboy" don't have a truly negative connotation.

Not only does Donnelly surprise us with the strong word choice, she also uses a lot of contrasting symbols. The unicorn could represent the male gaze, already predator-like, looking down on them. While they are sitting in the center of the rug, that looks very much like a target, or a never ending-cycle. The dolls may symbolize manipulation (the girls decide the dolls' futures the same way society decides their own). The fact that we can't see anything outside the window, regardless of it being open might mean that they can still not see how the world really is, but society is already looking at them. There is also the color scheme point. The constant use of pink and purple highlight innocence and the fact that we are talking about little girls the way they are viewed by society. This is very common in Donnelly's cartoons, which usually appear in the New Yorker, meant for an educated and liberal audience. She uses satire and colour, putting feminism always at the center of her work. She uses context to make the audience understand how bad the problem really is.

So… There is a clear setting here, and details give the audience a different perspective. And then there is the more important question, why does the little girl want to be a slut? What makes the idea of being a slut so attractive? The question sounds incongruent with the setting, but the simple answer is pretty obvious.

Every day, when she sees what society defines as a "good girl", she sees boring. A good girl that dresses "accordingly". A good girl has to act like a lady, sit with her legs crossed, not wear mini skirts. She has to obey. A good girl has to do so many things to still be considered a "good girl", the list is never ending. And of course it looks exhausting and confusing.

On the other hand, the little girls in the cartoon can see a free girl. A girl that sees the sky as the limit and has fun. A girl that does the same things her brother does but gets called slut instead of daring and adventurous like him. A "slut" wears makeup. She drives her own red, convertible car, goes wherever she wants. She chooses what to wear. She has friends that are guys, friends that are girls. She wears that strong red lipstick that looks so attractive to the little girl.

Everything that calls the little girl's attention has been connected for as long as she remembers with that amazing word … slut. So slut means for her, a wider door, a brighter life. Freedom. How can having control of your own life be sexualized? Life is so much more for a woman than just sex.
The safe and appropriate "good girls" ambience in the cartoon is actually setting very early chains on those girls who should like those colors, should play like that, should like unicorns. But of course she wants more.

Not following society's every rule and standard makes someone be seen as a girl who doesn't know how to be a proper girl. She's doing it wrong. And if she's doing it wrong, she must not be good. So what is a girl seen as when she makes her own decisions? A slut? Which takes us back to my first point. And I repeat, isn't it ironic how it all comes full circle?

What does this mean for those girls like the ones in the cartoon that turn into teenagers like the one in the poem that turn into women with sour stories to tell? What does it mean for the girls who want to take over the world, but are very confused on how to do it, because it's seen as wrong. Different is wrong, so they also confuse wrong with different, and that becomes a problem. As bad for them as for the world. And the problem itself is already shocking, because how can a little girl anywhere be sexualized in any way. And still that is our reality. And so it must change. Luckily, there are many girls that turn into teenagers that turn into women and they're working on it already.

10 bullet points

sexualization of girlhood by society. admirable and clear sighted women. 1999, 2011. Narrative poetry and symbolism. dramatic monologue. Past w/ contemporary. Fairytale language. spotted, just 16, vulnerable, justify, take advantage scarring. destination/goal. guessing... pace increased. young. trapped, free = had a choice. Now symbolism. Paperback-script.He,allegorical, predator,forest, clothes, 2 harsh phrases. His plan. would've been sexualized regardless sexualization at such an early age is what abruptly cut her now-buried childhood short. like Duffy, Donnelly's work ... Perspective. use of taboo language in striking ways. slut jumps out. shock factor. lawyer, doctor, pilot. Ironic - Full circle 'good' implications. or 'sluts'. sometimes clothes (dress-codes). Enforced by both. boys don't have this convo- manwhore. contrasting symbols. Male gaze, target, manipulation, window, color scheme - donnelly. NY (liberal). The question. Boring. accordingly. act like a lady, sit with her legs crossed, not wear mini skirts. she has to obey. vs free. car. Makeup having control be sexualized. early chains. proper girl or slut. full circle. little girls -> teens -> women sour stories. On it

10. EXAMPLE TEN (37/40)

Title: 'Expectations of masculinity: Marlboro Advertisement'

Author: Anonymous

Session: May 2023

Level: English A Lang and Lit SL

Literary text: *The Vegetarian*

Non-literary text: Marlboro advertisement

Global issue: Expectations of masculinity

Introduction:

- I will be exploring the global issue of the expectations of masculinity. I have selected *The Vegetarian* by Han Kang as the literary text and one of the Marlboro cigarette print advertisements as the non-literary text.

- The excerpt of *The Vegetarian* depicts the tension between Mr Cheong and Yeong-hye due to the latter's pursuit of a vegetarian diet. Mr Cheong is unable to understand his wife's decision and, later in the excerpt, resorts to violence to control her. The violence culminates in the scene of marital rape and it not only reflects the dominance of men in the family but also metaphorically alludes to patriarchy in Korean society. It is believed that the writer was deeply inspired by the Gwangju massacre in 1980, during which many pro-democratic demonstrators were killed by the military strongman Chun Doo-hwan.

- For the Marlboro print advertisement, the company attempts to associate its brand with dominant masculine qualities in cowboy culture to make its product more attractive to young male smokers. Both the setting of the rural landscape and the use of brown colour can be interpreted as signifiers of American male cowboy culture.

- Both texts depict the socially desired characteristics of masculinity. Although *The Vegetarian* is set in an East-Asian culture, and the Marlboro print advertisement in Western culture, the masculinity they represent shares some similarities.

Literary text:

To start with, I am exploring the global issue through the theme of **violence and dominance** in the extract from *The Vegetarian*. The novel is deeply entrenched in conservative Korean values, in which men exert multiple forms of violence on women and the family in exchange for obedience.

1. **P:** First Mr Cheong shows his emotional distance from his wife by saying:
   E: " I thought I could get by perfectly well just thinking of her as a stranger, or no, as a sister, or even a maid"
   A: Through the use of metaphor, it indicates that Mr Cheong sees his wife as a subservient minion. This implies Mr Cheong's desire to manipulate Yeong-hye. Also, the excerpt shows the vulnerability of their relationship due to Mr Cheong's reluctance to make efforts to understand her. The verb " get by" implies that Mr Cheong is unempathetic towards his wife, which accentuates the societal expectation that men should be emotionally tough.

2. **P:** Mr Cheong's use of sexual violence against Yeong-hye can be seen when he confesses
   E: "Pinning down her struggling arms and tugging her trousers"
   A: "Struggling arms" implies Yeong-hye's fight for autonomy. It is clear that Yeong-hye is resisting Mr Cheong's brutal manipulation, but Mr Cheong views this as an absurd form of disobedience. "Push" connotes thrusting and forcing, suggesting Mr Cheong's physical strength and direct control over Yeong-hye.

3. **P:** This issue can be continually explored when Mr Cheong proclaims that
   E: "As though she were a "comfort woman" dragged in against her will.
   A: By the use of metaphor, he highlights the dominance he has over Yeong-hye and her lack of body and sexual autonomy. This suggests that men are at the apex of the hierarchy in traditional Korean society, which justifies his actions. Here, the author criticizes the phenomenon of marital rape, whereby women are consumed by their husbands as commodities in an aggressive way.

Literary body of work:

The global issue of expectations of masculinity can also be explored through the theme of **violence and dominance** in other sections of *The Vegetarian*.

1. **P:** At the outset of the novel, Mr Cheong is introduced as a shiftless person as he states

   E: " I would marry the most run-of-the-mill woman in the world."

   A: Hence, the writer establishes the conventionality of the couple's existence, which highlights the ordinariness of violence and domination of males that can be seen as the novel progresses. The fact that he wants to marry a woman inferior to him suggests that he wishes to have a sense of superiority over his wife. This aligns with the general masculine expectation, which is for men to be superior to their wives.

2. **P:** Later in the novel, when Yeong-hye decides to abandon the meat after a gory dream, Mr Cheong is aggravated and finds her motivation inscrutable.

   E: He shouts " how could she be so self-centred"

   A: Through the use of the rhetorical question, the reader can develop an understanding of how irritated Mr Cheong is and his insecurity with Yeong-hye's unbothered attitude towards his anger. This shows the absolutist approach of men to judging and rationalising actions.

3. **P:** Lastly, not only does Mr Cheong dominate Yeong-hye physically, but her father also forces his wishes upon Yeong-hye in an aggressive and violent way. During the family gathering, Yeong-hye's father attempts to force-feed Yeong-hye a lump of meat.

   E: This can be seen when "he shook her off and thrust the pork at [my] wife's lips,"

   A: This suggests that he is authoritative and has the right to impose his own will on the family members. Linking back to the masculine expectations, the fact that he employs domestic violence against Yeong-hye in order to win obedience suggests the toughness of men.

Non-literary text:

Moving on to the non-literary text- the Marlboro print advertisement, I will explore the expectations of men through the **physical appearance and attitudes** of the male character in the print advertisement and the effects that the male character brings in terms of the marketing of cigarettes.

1. **P:** Firstly, the print advertisement features a herdsman, who expresses his charisma and attractiveness through facial features.
   E: Such features include thick eyebrows as well as a prominent nose symbolising the rugged physical expectations of men. His horse-riding position and his clothes seem to accentuate the charm of the character while identifying himself as a cowboy.
   A: These features aid the advertisement of cigarettes since these masculine qualities are appealing to males. Therefore, by consuming the product, the consumers envision themselves to be as virile as the model.

2. **P:** Furthermore, the attitude of the male character is portrayed to be powerful and strong.
   E: This can be seen when the male character is wearing a stetson hat and a brown denim jacket. The outfits of a cowboy suggest the tough condition and terrain of the area.
   A: This implies that he is a tough man who can survive the hardship and handle the situation. This aligns with the generalised masculine expectations since males are expected to be professional and independent. Moreover, the blurred background of the advertisement suggests there are vast quantities of horses, but the solitary man is able to dominate and control them. This shows his professionalism and his skills to manage the animals alone. All these qualities and merits are worshipped as desirable masculinities. Therefore, the target audience may be tempted by the strong mindset, which encourages them to purchase the product.

Non-literary body of work:

The male character in the overall Marlboro body of work is saturated with the qualities of masculinity. Coming back to the physical appearance of men, each and every print advertisement features an independent and handsome-looking cowboy, who embodies the ideal features and figure of men.

1. Each character has a strong physique and is portrayed to be intrepid. The settings of all the advertisements take place in a rustic paddock or in a rural place, which underscores the freedom and liberty associated with cigarettes. Furthermore, the use of the slogan " Come to Marlboro Country" utilizes metaphor and euphemism to encourage the target audience to pursue freedom. " Marlboro country" is a metaphor for the positive sensation while smoking cigarettes. This, thus, entices the smokers to appreciate the freedom that the company offers.

2. In addition to this, the main colours used in all the advertisements are brown and red, suggesting the dryness of the backdrop. The fact that all the backgrounds are similar in all advertisements suggests that Marlboro cigarettes are natural and organic. It also heightens the bucolic, yet toughness of the environment that the male characters have to endure alone, highlighting their masculine mentality and perseverance.

3. Last but not least, almost all the male characters are accompanied by horses. Horses are the main tools for transportation in cowboy culture. These images are mingled with excitement and uncertainties, which may align with the period of life for most young males. It also underscores the intrepid attitude that the cowboys have. All of the above characteristics contribute to the overall masculinity expectation. « Horse could symbolise to male prowess and strength. Taming a horse..tradition to show masculinity.

Conclusion:

In conclusion, although both texts depict the expectations of genders in a given society, they are different in terms of the goals and effects of the representation. *The Vegetarian* depicts masculinity through men's exertion of dominance over females and the family, the writer is thus criticising patriarchy and the overbearing manner of men. By contrast, the Marlboro advert capitalises on the desired qualities of masculinity to win consumers. Glorifies